NINJA BLAST MAX BLENDER
COOKBOOK FOR BEGINNERS
Easy Blending for Weight Loss, Energy & Meal Prep

Retta Buckridge

© copyright 2025 all right reserved

TABLE OF CONTENT

INTRODUCTION 7
GETTING STARTED WITH YOUR NINJA BLAST MAX BLENDER 8
BLENDER FUNCTIONS & FEATURES 8
APPETIZER RECIPES 10

1. Creamy Spinach Artichoke Dip 10
2. Garlic Parmesan White Bean Dip 10
3. Roasted Tomato Basil Bruschetta Spread ... 10
4. Smoky Chipotle Black Bean Dip 11
5. Creamy Tomato Basil Soup 11
6. Chilled Cucumber Yogurt Soup 11
7. Thai Spiced Butternut Squash Soup 11
8. Roasted Red Pepper & Carrot Soup 12
9. Zesty Corn & Avocado Soup 12
10. Garlic Mushroom Bisque 12
11. Broccoli Cheddar Blender Soup 13
12. Sweet Potato Ginger Soup 13
13. Vegan Cauliflower Curry Soup 13
14. Mini Caprese Skewers with Balsamic Glaze ... 13
15. Spicy Buffalo Cauliflower Bites 14
16. Sweet Potato & Black Bean Tostadas 14
17. Cheesy Spinach & Feta Phyllo Cups 15
18. Mediterranean Chickpea Patties 15
19. Savory Sun-Dried Tomato & Basil Bites 15
20. Smoky BBQ Lentil Sliders 15
21. Creamy Roasted Garlic Mashed Avocado ... 16
22. Silky Eggplant Baba Ganoush 16
23. Whipped Ricotta with Honey & Herbs 16
24. Tangy Greek Tzatziki Sauce 17
25. Vegan Cashew Cheese Spread 17
26. Carrot Ginger Miso Spread 17
27. Lemon Dill Feta Dip 18
28. Roasted Beet & Goat Cheese Spread 18
29. Zesty Cucumber Avocado Rolls 18
30. Thai Peanut Lettuce Wraps 18
31. Fresh Spring Rolls with Spicy Peanut Sauce ... 19
32. Avocado Toast with Pomegranate Seeds .. 19
33. Mango & Shrimp Ceviche 19
34. Greek Yogurt Ranch Veggie Dip 20
35. Asian Sesame Slaw Cups 20
36. Protein-packed edamame Hummus 20
37. Chilled Watermelon Basil Salad Cups 21
38. Tangy Pineapple Salsa with Baked Chips .. 21
39. Strawberry Coconut Chia Pudding 21
40. Mango Pineapple Salsa with Cinnamon Chips ... 22
41. Chocolate Almond Date Energy Bites 22
42. Creamy Peanut Butter Apple Dip 22
43. Raspberry Lemon Cheesecake Dip 23

BREAKFAST RECIPES 23

44. Banana Almond Power Smoothie 23
45. Classic Strawberry Banana Shake 23
46. Blueberry Oatmeal Smoothie 23
47. Peanut Butter Banana Protein Shake 24
48. Mango Pineapple Sunrise Smoothie 24
49. Green Detox Breakfast Smoothie 24
50. Chocolate Avocado Energy Shake 25
51. Vanilla Chia Protein Shake 25
52. Creamy Coffee Breakfast Shake 25
53. Tropical Coconut Mango Shake 25
54. Apple Cinnamon Breakfast Smoothie 26
55. Spinach and Pineapple Morning Blend 26
56. Pumpkin Spice Smoothie 26
57. Raspberry Oatmeal Shake 26

#	Recipe	Page	#	Recipe	Page
58.	Carrot Ginger Power Shake	27	77.	Greek Yogurt and Honey Smoothie	32
59.	Chocolate Peanut Butter Breakfast Shake	27	78.	Caramel Macchiato Protein Shake	33
60.	Pear and Almond Milk Smoothie	27	79.	Maple Walnut Oatmeal Smoothie	33
61.	Avocado and Matcha Protein Shake	28	80.	Dark Chocolate Berry Shake	33
62.	Blackberry Banana Blast	28	81.	Watermelon Mint Cooler	33
63.	Strawberry Cheesecake Smoothie	28	82.	Coconut Vanilla Shake	34
64.	Pomegranate Berry Antioxidant Shake	28	83.	Cinnamon Roll Smoothie	34
65.	Vanilla Pumpkin Pie Shake	29	84.	Chia Berry Protein Shake	34
66.	Pineapple Coconut Chia Shake	29	85.	Mocha Almond Butter Shake	35
67.	Choco-Banana Nut Shake	29	86.	Papaya Ginger Morning Drink	35
68.	Creamy Cashew Date Smoothie	30	87.	Banana Date Smoothie	35
69.	Orange Mango Energy Boost Smoothie	30	88.	Green Apple Kale Smoothie	35
70.	Raspberry Vanilla Yogurt Shake	30	89.	Cucumber Melon Refreshing Shake	36
71.	Apple Pie Smoothie	30	90.	Chocolate Cherry Almond Shake	36
72.	Coconut Matcha Latte Smoothie	31	91.	Vanilla Macadamia Shake	36
73.	High-Protein Coffee Shake	31	92.	Strawberry Oatmeal Shake	36
74.	Sweet Potato Breakfast Shake	31	93.	Lemon Blueberry Morning Bliss	37
75.	Honey Almond Breakfast Shake	32	94.	Choco-Coconut Power Shake	37
76.	Chocolate Hazelnut Morning Blend	32			

LUNCH RECIPES 37

#	Recipe	Page	#	Recipe	Page
95.	Nutty Banana Honey Smoothie	37	112.	Creamy Avocado Dressing	43
96.	Creamy Avocado Spinach Soup	38	113.	Thai Peanut Dipping Sauce	43
97.	Roasted Red Pepper & Tomato Soup	38	114.	Classic Caesar Dressing	43
98.	Classic Green Detox Smoothie	38	115.	Homemade Basil Pesto	43
99.	Mango Pineapple Protein Shake	39	116.	Roasted Garlic Hummus	44
100.	Strawberry Banana Oatmeal Smoothie	39	117.	Carrot Ginger Soup	44
101.	Creamy Peanut Butter Banana Shake	39	118.	Zucchini Basil Soup	44
102.	Iced Mocha Protein Shake	39	119.	Creamy Mushroom Soup	45
103.	Vegan Chocolate Almond Smoothie	40	120.	Choco-Banana Protein Pudding	45
104.	Spiced Pumpkin Pie Smoothie	40	121.	Matcha Coconut Smoothie	45
105.	Green Goddess Gazpacho	40	122.	Chilled Melon Mint Soup	46
106.	Butternut Squash & Carrot Soup	41	123.	Sun-Dried Tomato Hummus	46
107.	Tropical Mango Coconut Smoothie	41	124.	Pineapple Spinach Power Smoothie	46
108.	Creamy Sweet Corn Soup	41	125.	Blueberry Almond Butter Smoothie	47
109.	Mediterranean Hummus Dip	42	126.	Greek Yogurt Ranch Dressing	47
110.	Spicy Black Bean Soup	42	127.	Refreshing Watermelon Gazpacho	47
111.	Zesty Cilantro Lime Dressing	42	128.	Creamy Broccoli Cheddar Soup	47

#	Recipe	Page
129.	Almond Butter Date Energy Shake	48
130.	Apple Pie Protein Smoothie	48
131.	Honeydew Cucumber Cooler	48
132.	Creamy Roasted Cauliflower Soup	49
133.	Vegan Chocolate Mousse	49
134.	Chilled Avocado Lime Soup	49
135.	Creamy Coconut Carrot Soup	50
136.	Classic Tomato Basil Soup	50
137.	Lemon Tahini Dressing	50
138.	Roasted Beet Hummus	51
139.	Turmeric Golden Milk Smoothie	51
140.	Chocolate Peanut Butter Shake	51
141.	Cinnamon Apple Smoothie	51
142.	Berry Beet Power Smoothie	52
143.	Raspberry Chia Yogurt Bowl	52
144.	Creamy Cashew Tomato Soup	52
145.	Cucumber Avocado Gazpacho	53
146.	Sweet Potato Coconut Soup	53
147.	Spiced Mango Carrot Soup	53

DINNER RECIPES 54

#	Recipe	Page
148.	Butternut Squash & Apple Soup	54
149.	Broccoli Cheddar Soup	54
150.	Thai Coconut Curry Soup	54
151.	Roasted Red Pepper Soup	55
152.	Avocado Cilantro Soup	55
153.	Sweet Potato & Peanut Soup	55
154.	Blender Chicken Alfredo	56
155.	Creamy Pesto Pasta Sauce	56
156.	Zucchini & Walnut Pesto	56
157.	Spinach & Ricotta Stuffed Shells	57
158.	Vegan Cashew Cheese Sauce	57
159.	Spicy Roasted Tomato Salsa	57
160.	Blender Enchilada Sauce	58
161.	Creamy Garlic Parmesan Sauce	58
162.	Chipotle Lime Dressing	58
163.	Mango Habanero Salsa	59
164.	Blender Meatball Marinara	59
165.	Spaghetti with Blender Vodka Sauce	59
166.	Blender Bolognese Sauce	60
167.	Creamy Cajun Shrimp Pasta	60
168.	Chimichurri Marinated Steak	60
169.	Teriyaki Chicken Stir-Fry	61
170.	Thai Peanut Noodle Bowl	61
171.	Cashew Cream Vegan Alfredo	62
172.	Curried Lentil & Chickpea Bowl	62
173.	Creamy Sun-Dried Tomato Pasta	62
174.	Roasted Cauliflower & Garlic Soup	63
175.	Blender Pizza Sauce	63
176.	Vegan Mac & Cheese Sauce	63
177.	Spicy Blender Tofu Marinade	63
178.	Cilantro Lime Chicken Marinade	64
179.	Chipotle Ranch Dressing	64
180.	Italian Herb Blender Dressing	64
181.	Blender Gazpacho	65
182.	Korean BBQ Beef Marinade	65
183.	Garlic Butter Shrimp Pasta	65
184.	Greek Yogurt Tzatziki Sauce	66
185.	Avocado Ranch Dressing	66
186.	Lemon Herb Salmon Marinade	66
187.	Creamy Roasted Corn Soup	66
188.	Spiced Pumpkin Soup	67
189.	Buffalo Cauliflower Bites	67
190.	Mexican Street Corn Soup	68
191.	Coconut Mango Chicken Curry	68
192.	Blender Jerk Chicken Marinade	68
193.	Vegan Roasted Tomato Bisque	69
194.	Basil & Spinach Green Goddess Dressing	69
195.	Creamy Red Lentil Soup	69
196.	Blender Tandoori Chicken Marinade	70
197.	Honey Mustard Chicken Marinade	70
198.	Southwest Black Bean & Corn Soup	70

DESSERT RECIPES 70

199. Creamy Chocolate Mousse 71
200. Strawberry Cheesecake Shake 71
201. Blueberry Bliss Smoothie Bowl 71
202. Mango Coconut Pudding 71
203. Peanut Butter Banana Ice Cream 72
204. Raspberry Chia Pudding 72
205. Vanilla Bean Protein Shake 72
206. Chocolate Avocado Mousse 73
207. Tropical Pineapple Sorbet 73
208. Almond Butter Brownie Batter 73
209. Frozen Berry Yogurt Bark 74
210. Pumpkin Pie Smoothie 74
211. Matcha Green Tea Ice Cream 74
212. Chocolate Chip Cookie Dough Dip 74
213. Banana Oatmeal Mug Cake 75
214. Mocha Frappe Delight 75
215. Nutella Banana Whip 75
216. Salted Caramel Protein Shake 76
217. Blackberry Coconut Cream Bars 76
218. Chocolate Hazelnut Spread 76
219. Honey Almond Date Balls 77
220. Key Lime Pie Smoothie 77
221. Cinnamon Apple Crumble Shake 77
222. Espresso Chocolate Pudding 78
223. Pineapple Coconut Snow Cream 78
224. Frozen Strawberry Lemonade Slush 78
225. Dark Chocolate Raspberry Mousse 78
226. Protein-Packed Brownie Batter Dip 79
227. Gingerbread Cookie Smoothie 79
228. Carrot Cake Bliss Balls 79
229. Creamy Coconut Rice Pudding 80
230. Chocolate Covered Cherry Shake 80
231. Mango Passionfruit Sorbet 80
232. Oatmeal Raisin Cookie Dough Bites 81
233. Chocolate Covered Almond Shake 81
234. Peanut Butter Fudge Swirl 81
235. Lemon Blueberry Parfait 82
236. Chocolate Mint Chip Shake 82
237. Caramel Apple Pie Smoothie 82
238. Toasted Coconut Cream Shake 82
239. Chocolate Espresso Energy Balls 83
240. Vanilla Almond Butter Mousse 83
241. Dark Chocolate Peanut Butter Cups 83
242. Strawberry Shortcake Smoothie 84
243. Maple Pecan Pie Shake 84
244. Mocha Almond Fudge Ice Cream 84
245. Coconut Chia Pudding with Berries 84
246. White Chocolate Raspberry Swirl 85
247. Chocolate Covered Strawberry Mousse 85
248. Snickerdoodle Smoothie 85
249. Spiced Pumpkin Protein Pudding 86
250. Birthday Cake Blender Ice Cream 86
251. Chocolate Orange Mousse 86
252. Cherry Almond Bliss Shake 86
253. Caramel Mocha Fudge Shake 87

THE END 88

INTRODUCTION

With the Ninja Blast Max Blender, a strong and practical appliance that makes it simple to make scrumptious and nourishing beverages, sauces, and meals, blending has never been simpler. This cookbook will walk you through the fundamentals of making the most of your Ninja Blast Max Blender, regardless of your level of experience.

Packed with simple recipes that suit a range of dietary requirements and palates, this cookbook is ideal for beginners. You'll discover plenty of ideas to get the most out of your blender, from protein shakes and smoothies to soups, dips, sauces, and even desserts. Even someone with little culinary expertise may produce restaurant-caliber results in a matter of minutes with basic supplies and detailed instructions.

The Ninja Blast Max Blender's powerful blending skills are among its greatest features. This blender's high-speed blades make it easy to shatter ice, combine frozen fruits, and puree veggies until they're smooth. The Ninja Blast Max guarantees a flawless blend each and every time, whether you're creating a cool fruit sorbet, a velvety butternut squash soup, or a creamy peanut butter smoothie.

Along with helpful instructions on how to clean and maintain your blender, this cookbook also offers suggestions for item substitutions and combinations to help you become creative in the kitchen. There are also sections devoted to protein-rich dishes that promote an active lifestyle, detox beverages, and nutrient-dense smoothies if you're searching for healthy meal prep ideas.

This cookbook will help you get the most out of your Ninja Blast Max Blender, regardless of your level of expertise. Whether you're blending for convenience, health, or just fun, you'll quickly learn how simple it is to make delectable and fulfilling dishes in your own kitchen.

With the Ninja Blast Max Blender Cookbook for Beginners, let's get started and discover the world of blending!

GETTING STARTED WITH YOUR NINJA BLAST MAX BLENDER

It's crucial to get acquainted with your Ninja Blast Max Blender before beginning any recipe. What you should know is as follows:

❖ **Unboxing & Setup**

Carefully unpack all components: the blender base, blending jar, blade assembly, lid, and tamper.

Wash the blending jar and lid, and tamper with warm, soapy water before first use.

Place the blender on a flat, stable surface.

Attach the blending jar to the base, ensuring it locks securely.

Make sure the lid is tightly sealed before blending.

❖ **Safety Tips**

Before using the blender, make sure the lid is securely fastened.

Do not exceed the maximum fill line.

Use the tamper only when the lid is securely in place.

Avoid blending hot liquids unless specifically designed for heat-safe blending.

To avoid residue accumulation, always clean the blender right away after using it.

BLENDER FUNCTIONS & FEATURES

With its strong blending powers and pre-programmed features, the Ninja Blast Max Blender will simplify your culinary experience. The salient aspects are as follows:

❖ **High-Speed Motor**

A powerful motor ensures smooth and efficient blending of tough ingredients like ice, nuts, and fibrous vegetables.

❖ **Multiple Speed Settings & Pulse Function**

Adjustable speed levels allow you to control texture and consistency.

In order to chop or break down components without over-blending, the pulse mode offers brief power spurts.

❖ **Pre-Programmed Blending Modes**
- **Smoothie Mode** – Perfect for creamy and well-blended smoothies.
- **Ice Crush Mode** – Designed to break down ice and freeze fruits effortlessly.
- **Soup Mode** – Warms and blends soups directly in the jar (if heat-safe).
- **Nut Butter Mode** – A dedicated setting for making homemade peanut butter, almond butter, and more.

❖ **Easy-to-Clean Design**

Dishwasher-safe components make cleanup a breeze.

The self-cleaning mode allows for quick rinsing—just add warm water & a drop of dish soap, then blend for a few seconds.

❖ **Travel-Friendly & Compact**

Ideal for small kitchens, dorms, and on-the-go lifestyles.

Portable blending jar options make it easy to take your smoothies with you.

APPETIZER RECIPES

1. Creamy Spinach Artichoke Dip

Total Time: 15 minutes | Prep Time: 10 minutes | Cook Time: 5 minutes

Ingredients:

- 1 cup canned artichoke hearts, drained
- 1 cup fresh spinach, chopped
- ½ cup cream cheese, softened
- ¼ cup sour cream
- ¼ cup grated Parmesan cheese
- 1 clove garlic, minced
- ½ teaspoon salt
- ¼ teaspoon black pepper

Directions:

a) In the blender, combine the spinach, sour cream, cream cheese, Parmesan, and artichoke hearts. b) Add salt, black pepper, and chopped garlic. c) Using a scraper, if necessary, blend until smooth and creamy. d) Over medium heat, transfer the mixture to a small saucepan. e) Cook until heated and slightly thickened, stirring regularly, for 5 minutes. f) The dish should be served immediately with crackers or toasted bread.

2. Garlic Parmesan White Bean Dip

Total Time: 10 minutes | Prep Time: 10 minutes

Ingredients:

- 1 can (15 oz) cannellini beans, drained and rinsed
- 2 cloves garlic, minced
- ¼ cup grated Parmesan cheese
- ¼ cup olive oil
- 2 tablespoons lemon juice
- ½ teaspoon salt
- ¼ teaspoon black pepper
- ¼ teaspoon paprika (optional)

Directions:

a) In the blender, combine the cannellini beans, lemon juice, olive oil, Parmesan cheese, and garlic. b) Add paprika, if using, and salt and black pepper. c) Blend until smooth, pausing as necessary to scrape down the edges. d) To get the correct consistency, thin the dip with a tablespoon of water or olive oil if it's too thick. e) As necessary, taste and adjust the seasoning. f) Before serving, move to a serving dish and brush with more olive oil.

3. Roasted Tomato Basil Bruschetta Spread

Total Time: 20 minutes | Prep Time: 5 minutes | Cook Time: 15 minutes

Ingredients:

- 2 cups cherry tomatoes, halved
- 2 tablespoons olive oil
- 2 cloves garlic, minced
- ¼ teaspoon salt
- ¼ teaspoon black pepper
- ¼ teaspoon red pepper flakes (optional)
- ¼ cup fresh basil leaves
- 1 tablespoon balsamic vinegar

Directions:

a) Turn the oven on to 400°F or 200°C. b) Ingredients such as salt, black pepper, red pepper flakes, garlic, olive oil, and cherry tomatoes should be added. c) Place on a baking sheet and bake for fifteen minutes or until it reaches the desired tenderness and tastes slightly caramelized. d) Add the roasted tomatoes to the blender. e) Add balsamic vinegar and fresh basil leaves. f) Depending on your choice, blend until it's smooth or somewhat lumpy. g) Serve warm or cold with pieces of toasted bread.

4. Smoky Chipotle Black Bean Dip

Total Time: 10 minutes | Prep Time: 10 minutes

Ingredients:

1 can (15 oz) black beans, drained	1 chipotle pepper in adobo sauce
1 clove garlic, minced	2 tablespoons lime juice
¼ teaspoon smoked paprika	½ teaspoon salt
¼ teaspoon black pepper	2 tablespoons olive oil
2 tablespoons water (if needed)	

Directions:

a) In the blender, combine black beans, smoked paprika, lime juice, chipotle pepper, garlic, salt, and black pepper. b) Pour some olive oil over it. c) Add water as necessary to alter the consistency after blending until smooth. d) If needed, taste and adjust the seasoning. e) Move to a bowl and serve with fresh vegetables or tortilla chips.

5. Creamy Tomato Basil Soup

Total Time: 15 minutes | Prep Time: 5 minutes

Ingredients:

3 large tomatoes, chopped	1/2 cup vegetable broth
1/2 cup heavy cream or coconut milk	1/4 cup fresh basil leaves
1 clove garlic, minced	1/2 teaspoon salt
1/4 teaspoon black pepper	

Directions:

a) Fill the Ninja Blast Max Blender with chopped tomatoes, vegetable broth, and minced garlic. b) Smoothly blend on high. c) After transferring the mixture to a saucepan, cook it for five minutes over medium heat. d) Add coconut milk or heavy cream and season with salt and pepper. e) To get a smooth texture, put the mixture back in the blender and blend one more. f) Transfer into dishes and sprinkle with fresh basil leaves for garnish. Warm up and serve.

6. Chilled Cucumber Yogurt Soup

Total Time: 10 minutes | Prep Time: 5 minutes

Ingredients:

1 large cucumber, peeled and chopped	1 cup plain Greek yogurt
1/2 cup cold water	2 tablespoons fresh dill, chopped
1 small garlic clove, minced	1 tablespoon lemon juice
1/2 teaspoon salt	1/4 teaspoon black pepper

Directions:

a) In the blender, combine the cucumber, Greek yoghurt, water, lemon juice, dill, and garlic. b) On high, blend until creamy and smooth. c) Season with salt and black pepper after tasting. d) Add the spice and blend again for a few seconds. e) Before serving, let it sit in the refrigerator for at least half an hour. f) Transfer to bowls and top with cucumber slices or more dill. Serve cold.

7. Thai Spiced Butternut Squash Soup

Total Time: 20 minutes | Prep Time: 5 minutes

Ingredients:

2 cups cooked butternut squash	1 cup coconut milk
1/2 cup vegetable broth	1 tablespoon red curry paste
1 teaspoon grated ginger	1 clove garlic, minced

1/2 teaspoon salt	1/4 teaspoon black pepper

Directions:

a) In the blender, combine the cooked butternut squash, curry paste, ginger, garlic, coconut milk, and vegetable broth. b) Blend until the mixture is absolutely smooth. c) After pouring the mixture into a saucepan, cook it for five to seven minutes over medium heat. d) Salt and pepper should be added, and the seasoning should be adjusted as required. e) For an extra creamy texture, blend again. f) Garnish with fresh cilantro or a coconut milk swirl, and serve warm.

8. Roasted Red Pepper & Carrot Soup

Total Time: 15 minutes | Prep Time: 5 minutes

Ingredients:

2 roasted red bell peppers, peeled	1 large carrot, peeled and chopped
1 cup vegetable broth	1/2 cup coconut milk
1 teaspoon smoked paprika	1 clove garlic, minced
1/2 teaspoon salt	1/4 teaspoon black pepper

Directions:

a) Put the carrot, vegetable broth, garlic, and roasted red peppers in the blender. b) Smoothly blend on high. c) After pouring the mixture into a saucepan, cook it for five minutes over medium heat. d) Stir in coconut milk, smoked paprika, salt, and pepper. e) For a silky texture, blend once more. f) Garnish with croutons or fresh parsley and serve warm.

9. Zesty Corn & Avocado Soup

Total Time: 10 minutes | Prep Time: 5 minutes

Ingredients:

1 cup corn kernels (fresh or frozen)	1 ripe avocado, peeled and pitted
1/2 cup vegetable broth	1/2 cup coconut milk
1 tablespoon lime juice	1/2 teaspoon cumin
1/2 teaspoon salt	1/4 teaspoon black pepper

Directions:

a) In the blender, combine the corn, avocado, coconut milk, and vegetable broth. b) Blend until smooth and creamy. c) Add salt, black pepper, cumin, and lime juice and stir. d) You should then add the spices and mix for a few more seconds. e) Serve right away or refrigerate for 20 minutes to make a cool soup. f) Before serving, garnish with more corn kernels and fresh cilantro.

10. Garlic Mushroom Bisque

Total Time: 25 minutes | Prep Time: 10 minutes

Ingredients:

2 cups cremini mushrooms, sliced	2 cloves garlic, minced
1 small onion, chopped	2 cups vegetable broth
1 cup heavy cream	1 tbsp olive oil
1 tsp thyme	Salt and pepper to taste

Directions:

a) Melt the olive oil in a saucepan by heating it over a medium flame. Add the garlic and onions and sauté until aromatic. b) Cook the thyme and mushrooms until they are tender. c) For ten minutes, boil the vegetable broth after adding it. d) After letting the mixture cool a little, pour it into the Ninja Blast Max Blender. e) Blend till creamy and smooth. f) Put everything back in the saucepan, add the heavy cream, and simmer it for two more minutes. g) To taste, add salt and pepper. h) Garnish with fresh thyme and serve warm.

11. Broccoli Cheddar Blender Soup

Total Time: 20 minutes | Prep Time: 10 minutes

Ingredients:

- 2 cups broccoli florets, steamed
- 1 small carrot, diced
- 2 cups vegetable broth
- 1 tbsp butter
- 1 cup shredded cheddar cheese
- 1 small onion, chopped
- 1 cup milk (or non-dairy alternative)
- Salt and pepper to taste

Directions:

a) The carrots and onions should be cooked in a pan with butter that has been melted over medium heat until they are firm. b) Cook for five minutes after adding the vegetable broth and cooked broccoli. c) After letting the mixture cool a little, pour it into the Ninja Blast Max Blender. d) Blend until it's smooth. e) Put back in the saucepan and mix in the shredded cheddar and milk. f) Continue to heat for 3–4 more minutes until the cheese is completely melted. g) Add salt and pepper for seasoning. h) Top with more cheese and serve warm.

12. Sweet Potato Ginger Soup

Total Time: 30 minutes | Prep Time: 10 minutes

Ingredients:

- 2 cups sweet potatoes, peeled and diced
- 2 cloves garlic, minced
- 2 cups vegetable broth
- 1 tbsp olive oil
- 1 small onion, chopped
- 1-inch fresh ginger, grated
- 1 cup coconut milk
- Salt and pepper to taste

Directions:

a) Olive oil should be heated in a saucepan over medium heat, and then the ginger, garlic, and onions should be cooked in the oil. b) Simmer the vegetable broth and sweet potatoes for 15 minutes or until they are soft. c) After letting the mixture cool a little, pour it into the Ninja Blast Max Blender. d) Blend till creamy and smooth. e) Pour the coconut milk back into the saucepan and stir. f) For two to three more minutes, heat. g) Add salt and pepper for seasoning. h) Garnish with fresh herbs and serve warm.

13. Vegan Cauliflower Curry Soup

Total Time: 25 minutes | Prep Time: 10 minutes

Ingredients:

- 2 cups cauliflower florets
- 2 cloves garlic, minced
- 1/2 tsp turmeric
- 1 cup coconut milk
- Salt and pepper to taste
- 1 small onion, chopped
- 1 tsp curry powder
- 2 cups vegetable broth
- 1 tbsp olive oil

Directions:

a) In a skillet with heated olive oil, sauté the garlic and onions until they are tender. b) Cook for 3–4 minutes after adding the cauliflower, curry powder, and turmeric. c) After adding the vegetable broth, cook the cauliflower for ten minutes or until it is soft. d) After letting the mixture cool a little, pour it into the Ninja Blast Max Blender. e) Blend until it's smooth. f) Put back in the saucepan, add the coconut milk, and cook for three more minutes. g) Add salt and pepper for seasoning. h) Garnish with fresh cilantro and serve warm.

14. Mini Caprese Skewers with Balsamic Glaze

Total Time: 10 minutes | Prep Time: 10 minutes

Ingredients:

12 cherry tomatoes	12 mini mozzarella balls
12 fresh basil leaves	2 tbsp balsamic glaze
1 tbsp olive oil	Salt and pepper to taste
12 small skewers	

Directions:

a) On each skewer, thread a cherry tomato. b) Add a little mozzarella ball and a fresh basil leaf after that. c) Continue until every skewer is put together. d) Pour some olive oil over it. e) Add salt and pepper sparingly. f) Drizzle the skewers with balsamic glaze. g) Serve right away.

15. Spicy Buffalo Cauliflower Bites

Total Time: 30 minutes | Prep Time: 10 minutes

Ingredients:

2 cups cauliflower florets	½ cup almond flour
½ cup water	1 teaspoon garlic powder
1 teaspoon onion powder	½ teaspoon smoked paprika
½ teaspoon salt	½ teaspoon black pepper
½ cup buffalo sauce	1 tablespoon melted butter

Directions:

a) Put parchment paper on a baking pan and preheat the oven to 400°F (200°C). b) Almond flour, water, paprika, onion powder, garlic powder, salt, and pepper should all be blended into a homogeneous batter in the Ninja Blast Max Blender. c) Make sure the cauliflower florets are well covered by dipping them into the batter. d) After lining the baking sheet with the coated florets, bake them for twenty minutes, flipping them over midway through the cooking process. e) Meanwhile, use a blender to smooth up the buffalo sauce and melted butter. f) Take the cauliflower out of the oven, mix it with the buffalo sauce, and then put it back in for five more minutes. g) Before serving, let it cool somewhat. Serve with blue cheese or ranch dressing.

16. Sweet Potato & Black Bean Tostadas

Total Time: 35 minutes | Prep Time: 10 minutes

Ingredients:

1 large sweet potato, peeled and diced	1 cup black beans, drained and rinsed
½ teaspoon cumin	½ teaspoon chilli powder
½ teaspoon salt	1 tablespoon lime juice
4 small corn tortillas	½ cup shredded lettuce
¼ cup diced tomatoes	¼ cup crumbled cotija cheese
2 tablespoons sour cream	

Directions:

a) Put parchment paper on a baking pan and preheat the oven to 400°F (200°C). b) Almond flour, water, paprika, onion powder, garlic powder, salt, and pepper should all be blended into a homogeneous batter in the Ninja Blast Max Blender. c) Make sure the cauliflower florets are well covered by dipping them into the batter. d) After lining the baking sheet with the coated florets, bake them for twenty minutes, flipping them over midway through the cooking process. e) Meanwhile, use a blender to smooth up the buffalo sauce and melted butter. f) Take the cauliflower out of the oven, mix it with the buffalo sauce, and then put it back in for five more minutes. g) Before serving, let it cool somewhat. Serve with blue cheese or ranch dressing.

17. Cheesy Spinach & Feta Phyllo Cups

Total Time: 25 minutes | Prep Time: 10 minutes

Ingredients:

1 cup fresh spinach	½ cup feta cheese
¼ cup ricotta cheese	1 egg
½ teaspoon garlic powder	½ teaspoon black pepper
12 mini phyllo cups	

Directions:

a) For 375 degrees Fahrenheit (190 degrees Celsius), preheat the oven. b) Blend spinach, feta, ricotta, egg, black pepper, and garlic powder in the Ninja Blast Max Blender until smooth. c) Place the cups of phyllo on a baking sheet. d) Evenly fill each phyllo cup with spinach mixture using a spoon. e) The filling should be set and faintly browned after 12 to 15 minutes in the oven. f) Before serving, let it cool for a few minutes.

18. Mediterranean Chickpea Patties

Total Time: 30 minutes | Prep Time: 10 minutes

Ingredients:

1 can (15 oz) chickpeas, drained and rinsed	½ cup rolled oats
1 small onion, chopped	1 garlic clove, minced
1 teaspoon cumin	½ teaspoon paprika
½ teaspoon salt	2 tablespoons lemon juice
2 tablespoons olive oil	

Directions:

a) Mix the chickpeas, oats, onion, garlic, cumin, paprika, salt, and lemon juice in the Ninja Blast Max Blender until a thick consistency is achieved. b) Create little patties out of the mixture. c) In a pan, heat the olive oil over medium heat. d) Cook the patties until golden brown, 4–5 minutes each side. e) Serve with hummus or tzatziki.

19. Savory Sun-Dried Tomato & Basil Bites

Total Time: 25 minutes | Prep Time: 10 minutes

Ingredients:

½ cup sun-dried tomatoes	1 cup chickpeas, drained and rinsed
½ cup almonds	¼ cup fresh basil leaves
1 tablespoon lemon juice	½ teaspoon salt
¼ teaspoon black pepper	1 tablespoon olive oil

Directions:

a) Sun-dried tomatoes, chickpeas, almonds, basil, lemon juice, salt, and pepper should all be blended until smooth in the Ninja Blast Max Blender. b) Create little, bite-sized balls out of the mixture by rolling it. c) In a pan, heat the olive oil over medium heat. d) The bites should be pan-fried lightly for two to three minutes on each side. e) Warm or room temperature, serve.

20. Smoky BBQ Lentil Sliders

Total Time: 30 minutes | Prep Time: 10 minutes

Ingredients:

1 cup cooked lentils	½ cup breadcrumbs
¼ cup BBQ sauce	1 teaspoon smoked paprika
½ teaspoon garlic powder	½ teaspoon onion powder

½ teaspoon salt	1 tablespoon flaxseed meal + 3 tablespoons water (flax egg)
1 tablespoon olive oil	6 mini slider buns
Lettuce, tomato slices, and pickles for serving	

Directions:

a) A small dish should be used to combine the flaxseed meal and water, and then it should be left for five minutes. b) In the Ninja Blast Max Blender, combine the lentils, breadcrumbs, BBQ sauce, smoked paprika, onion powder, garlic powder, and salt. Blend until well mixed but still has some chunks. c) Stir the flax egg into the mixture after pouring it into a bowl. Give the mixture five minutes to rest. d) Make little patties that are about the size of slider buns. e) The patties should be cooked in a pan set over medium heat with heated olive oil for three to four minutes on each side or until they have a golden brown colour. f) After toasting the slider buns, top with more BBQ sauce, pickles, lettuce, and tomato slices. g) Warm-up and dig in!

21. Creamy Roasted Garlic Mashed Avocado

Total Time: 15 minutes | Prep Time: 5 minutes

Ingredients:

2 ripe avocados	1 head roasted garlic (about six cloves)
1 tablespoon lemon juice	2 tablespoons Greek yogurt
½ teaspoon salt	¼ teaspoon black pepper
1 teaspoon olive oil	

Directions:

a) Scoop the flesh into the Ninja Blast Max Blender after halving the avocados and removing the pits. b) The roasted garlic cloves should be squeezed into the blender. c) Add Greek yoghurt, lemon juice, black pepper, and salt. d) Combine, being sure to scrape down the sides as needed, until the mixture is silky smooth and creamy. e) Stir the mixture for an additional five seconds after adding a drizzle of olive oil. f) Serve right away as a toast spread or dip.

22. Silky Eggplant Baba Ganoush

Total Time: 40 minutes | Prep Time: 10 minutes

Ingredients:

1 large eggplant	2 tablespoons tahini
2 tablespoons lemon juice	2 garlic cloves
1 teaspoon cumin	½ teaspoon smoked paprika
½ teaspoon salt	2 tablespoons olive oil

Directions:

a) Set the oven's temperature to 400°F or 200°C. After halving the eggplant, roast it for 30 minutes to make it tender. b) After the eggplant has cooled, remove the flesh with a spoon and place it in the Ninja Blast Max Blender. c) Add salt, smoked paprika, cumin, garlic, lemon juice, and tahini. d) After adding the olive oil, whisk the mixture until it is thoroughly combined and has a creamy consistency. e) As necessary, taste and adjust the seasoning. f) Serve with fresh vegetables or pita bread.

23. Whipped Ricotta with Honey & Herbs

Total Time: 10 minutes | Prep Time: 5 minutes

Ingredients:

1 cup ricotta cheese	1 tablespoon honey
1 tablespoon olive oil	½ teaspoon salt
½ teaspoon black pepper	1 teaspoon fresh thyme or rosemary

1 teaspoon lemon zest

Directions:

a) Fill the Ninja Blast Max Blender with ricotta cheese, honey, olive oil, salt, black pepper, and lemon zest. b) Continue to blend for about thirty seconds or until the mixture is smooth and fluffy. If necessary, taste and adjust the sweetness or seasoning. c) Place the mixture in a serving dish and top with fresh thyme or rosemary just before serving. d) Before serving, drizzle some more honey over it. e) Serve with fresh fruit, crostini, or crackers.

24. Tangy Greek Tzatziki Sauce

Total Time: 15 minutes | Prep Time: 10 minutes

Ingredients:

1 cup Greek yogurt	½ cucumber, grated and squeezed dry
1 tablespoon lemon juice	1 garlic clove
1 teaspoon olive oil	½ teaspoon salt
½ teaspoon dried dill	¼ teaspoon black pepper

Directions:

a) Using a paper towel, squeeze off any extra moisture after grating the cucumber. b) Fill the Ninja Blast Max Blender with Greek yoghurt, lemon juice, olive oil, garlic, salt, dill, and black pepper. c) Blend till creamy and smooth. d) Add the grated cucumber and stir. e) Spoon into a bowl and refrigerate for ten minutes or longer. f) Serve as a sauce or dip for veggies, pita bread, or grilled meats.

25. Vegan Cashew Cheese Spread

Total Time: 15 minutes | Prep Time: 10 minutes

Ingredients:

1 cup raw cashews	2 tbsp nutritional yeast
1 tbsp lemon juice	1 tsp apple cider vinegar
1/2 tsp garlic powder	1/2 tsp onion powder
1/2 tsp salt	1/4 cup water (adjust as needed)

Directions:

a) After soaking, drain and rinse the cashews. b) Fill the Ninja Blast Max Blender with all of the ingredients. c) Scrape down the edges as necessary and blend on high speed until smooth. d) One tablespoon of water at a time may be added to the mixture if it's too thick until the right consistency is achieved. e) If necessary, taste and adjust the seasoning. f) Before serving, move to an airtight container and chill for at least half an hour. g) Use as a spread for vegetables, sandwiches, and crackers. h) Keep in the refrigerator for up to five days.

26. Carrot Ginger Miso Spread

Total Time: 15 minutes | Prep Time: 10 minutes

Ingredients:

1 cup cooked carrots (steamed or boiled)	2 tbsp white miso paste
1 tbsp fresh ginger, minced	1 tbsp rice vinegar
1 tbsp sesame oil	1/2 tsp garlic powder
1/4 tsp salt	2 tbsp water (adjust as needed)

Directions:

a) Fill the Ninja Blast Max Blender with all of the ingredients. b) Blend, scraping down sides as necessary, until smooth. c) If it's too thick, thin it out by adding a tablespoon of water at a time. d) If necessary, taste and adjust the vinegar or salt.

27. Lemon Dill Feta Dip

Total Time: 10 minutes | Prep Time: 5 minutes

Ingredients:

1 cup crumbled feta cheese	1/2 cup Greek yogurt
1 tbsp lemon juice	1 tsp lemon zest
1 tbsp fresh dill, chopped	1 small garlic clove, minced
1 tbsp olive oil	1/4 tsp black pepper

Directions:

a) Fill the Ninja Blast Max Blender with all of the ingredients. b) Blend till creamy and smooth on medium speed. c) If necessary, scrape down the edges and combine once more. d) If needed, taste and adjust the seasoning. e) Pour more olive oil over it after transferring it to a bowl. f) To bring out the flavours, let it rest for ten minutes. g) Serve with fresh vegetables, crackers, or pita chips. h) Keep in the refrigerator for up to five days.

28. Roasted Beet & Goat Cheese Spread

Total Time: 20 minutes | Prep Time: 10 minutes

Ingredients:

1 cup roasted beets, peeled and chopped	1/2 cup goat cheese
1 tbsp honey	1 tbsp balsamic vinegar
1 tbsp olive oil	1/4 tsp salt
1/4 tsp black pepper	

Directions:

a) Fill the Ninja Blast Max Blender with all of the ingredients. b) Blend, scraping down the sides as necessary, until smooth and creamy. c) If desired, add extra vinegar or honey after tasting and adjusting the seasoning. d) After transferring, refrigerate for 15 minutes in a serving dish. e) Serve as a sandwich spread or with crostini or crackers. f) Add more chopped nuts or crumbled goat cheese as a garnish. g) Keep in the refrigerator for up to 4 days in an airtight container. h) Savour it as a spread or dip!

29. Zesty Cucumber Avocado Rolls

Total Time: 15 minutes | Prep Time: 10 minutes

Ingredients:

1 ripe avocado	1/2 cucumber, diced
1 tbsp lemon juice	1 tbsp fresh cilantro, chopped
1/2 tsp garlic powder	1/4 tsp salt
1/4 tsp black pepper	6 thin cucumber slices for rolling

Directions:

a) Fill the Ninja Blast Max Blender with the following Ingredients: avocado, chopped cucumber, lemon juice, cilantro, garlic powder, salt, and pepper. b) Blend till creamy and smooth. c) As necessary, taste and adjust the seasoning. d) On a level board, arrange thin slices of cucumber. e) On each slice, spread a little bit of the avocado mixture. f) Roll each slice of cucumber carefully, and if necessary, fasten with a toothpick. g) Before serving, arrange on a dish and refrigerate for five minutes. h) Savour this nutritious and revitalizing appetizer!

30. Thai Peanut Lettuce Wraps

Total Time: 20 minutes | Prep Time: 15 minutes

Ingredients:

1/2 cup peanut butter	2 tbsp soy sauce
1 tbsp honey	1 tbsp rice vinegar
1 tsp sesame oil	1 clove garlic, minced
1/2 tsp ginger, minced	1/4 cup water (adjust for consistency)
1 lb ground chicken or tofu	1 cup shredded carrots
1/2 cup chopped red bell pepper	1/4 cup chopped cilantro
8 butter lettuce leaves	

Directions:

a) Peanut butter, soy sauce, honey, rice vinegar, sesame oil, ginger, garlic, and water should all be blended until smooth in the Ninja Blast Max Blender. b) The ground chicken or tofu should be cooked in a skillet over medium heat until it can be browned and cooked all the way through. c) After the red bell pepper and shredded carrots have been added to the pan, stir the mixture for a period of two minutes. d) Take off the heat and stir in the cilantro. e) Spoon the mixture into the leaves of the lettuce. f) Serve right away with a drizzle of peanut sauce.

31. Fresh Spring Rolls with Spicy Peanut Sauce

Total Time: 25 minutes | Prep Time: 20 minutes

Ingredients:

8 rice paper wrappers	1 cup cooked shrimp, sliced in half lengthwise
1/2 cup shredded carrots	1/2 cup julienned cucumber
1/2 cup red bell pepper, thinly sliced	1/4 cup fresh mint leaves
1/4 cup fresh basil leaves	1/4 cup fresh cilantro leaves

Spicy Peanut Sauce:

1/2 cup peanut butter	2 tbsp soy sauce
1 tbsp sriracha	1 tbsp honey
1 clove garlic, minced	1/4 cup water

Directions:

a) Using the Ninja Blast Max Blender, blend all of the sauce components until they are smooth. Put aside. b) The rice paper wrapper should be soaked in warm water for a few seconds in order to make it more pliable. c) Arrange the shrimp, carrots, cucumber, red bell pepper, and fresh herbs in the middle of the wrapper, which should be laid down flat. d) Tightly roll from the bottom up after folding the sides inside. e) Continue with the rest of the wrappers. f) Serve each roll with spicy peanut sauce after slicing it in half.

32. Avocado Toast with Pomegranate Seeds

Total Time: 10 minutes | Prep Time: 5 minutes

Ingredients:

1 ripe avocado	1 tbsp lemon juice
1/2 tsp sea salt	1/4 tsp black pepper
2 slices whole-grain bread	2 tbsp pomegranate seeds
1 tsp olive oil	1/2 tsp red pepper flakes (optional)

Directions:

a) Blend the avocado, lemon juice, salt, and pepper in the Ninja Blast Max Blender until they are creamy. b) The whole-grain bread should be toasted until golden brown. c) On each slice, equally distribute the avocado mixture. d) Olive oil should be drizzled on top, and pomegranate seeds should be mixed in. e) For added spice, you may optionally add red pepper flakes. f) Enjoy right away after serving.

33. Mango & Shrimp Ceviche

Total Time: 30 minutes | Prep Time: 15 minutes

Ingredients:

- 1/2 lb cooked shrimp, chopped
- 1 ripe mango, diced
- 1/2 red onion, finely chopped
- 1/2 cup cherry tomatoes, halved
- 1/4 cup fresh cilantro, chopped
- 1 jalapeño, finely diced
- Juice of 2 limes
- 1/2 tsp sea salt
- 1/4 tsp black pepper

Directions:

a) Blend half of the mango and lime juice in the Ninja Blast Max Blender until smooth. b) Add the shrimp, red onion, cherry tomatoes, cilantro, jalapeño, and chopped mango to a mixing bowl. c) Cover the ceviche with the blended mango-lime sauce and well combine. d) Add salt and pepper for seasoning. e) To let the flavours blend, cover and chill for 15 minutes. f) Serve cold on lettuce cups or with tortilla chips.

34. Greek Yogurt Ranch Veggie Dip

Total Time: 10 minutes | Prep Time: 5 minutes

Ingredients:

- 1 cup Greek yogurt
- 1 tbsp lemon juice
- 1 tsp dried dill
- 1 tsp garlic powder
- 1 tsp onion powder
- 1/2 tsp salt
- 1/2 tsp black pepper
- 1 tbsp chopped fresh parsley
- 1 tbsp chopped chives

Directions:

a) Fill the Ninja Blast Max Blender with all of the ingredients. b) Blend till creamy and smooth. c) Move to a bowl and leave for five minutes. d) Add more parsley and chives as garnish. e) Serve with bell peppers, cucumbers, and carrots, all of which should be freshly chopped.

35. Asian Sesame Slaw Cups

Total Time: 15 minutes | Prep Time: 15 minutes

Ingredients:

- 2 cups shredded cabbage (red or green)
- 1 small carrot, julienned
- 1/4 cup chopped cilantro
- 2 green onions, chopped
- 1 tablespoon sesame seeds
- 1 tablespoon soy sauce
- 1 tablespoon rice vinegar
- 1 teaspoon sesame oil
- 1 teaspoon honey
- 6 mini lettuce cups (butter or romaine)

Directions:

a) Fill the Ninja Blast Max Blender with soy sauce, rice vinegar, sesame oil, and honey. Mix until well blended. b) Combine the green onions, sesame seeds, cilantro, cabbage, and carrots in a big bowl. c) Toss the slaw well after adding the combined dressing. d) Give the slaw five minutes to steep in the flavours. e) Place the cups of lettuce on a platter. f) The sesame slaw should be poured into each lettuce cup. g) Top with more sesame seeds. h) Serve right away and savour!

36. Protein-packed edamame Hummus

Total Time: 10 minutes | Prep Time: 10 minutes

Ingredients:

- 1 cup cooked edamame
- 2 tablespoons tahini
- 2 tablespoons lemon juice
- 1 garlic clove
- 1 tablespoon olive oil
- 1/2 teaspoon salt
- 1/2 teaspoon ground cumin
- 3 tablespoons water (as needed)

Directions:

a) Fill the Ninja Blast Max Blender with all the contents except water. b) Add water a little at a time to alter consistency after blending until smooth. c) To get a creamy texture, scrape down the edges and combine one more. d) If necessary, taste and add additional salt or lemon juice to adjust the seasoning. e) Pour more olive oil over it after transferring it to a bowl. f) Sprinkle sesame seeds or cumin on top as a garnish. g) Serve with vegetable sticks, crackers, or pita chips. h) You may keep leftovers in the refrigerator for up to three days.

37. Chilled Watermelon Basil Salad Cups

Total Time: 10 minutes | Prep Time: 10 minutes

Ingredients:

- 2 cups seedless watermelon, diced
- 1/2 cup cucumber, diced
- 1/2 teaspoon honey
- 1/4 cup fresh basil leaves
- 1 tablespoon lime juice
- 6 mini lettuce cups (butter or romaine)

Directions:

a) In the Ninja Blast Max Blender, combine the basil, lime juice, and honey. Blend until it's smooth. b) Combine the chopped cucumber and watermelon in a bowl. c) Over the mixture, drizzle the basil-lime dressing and toss gently. d) Place the cups of lettuce on a platter. e) Fill each lettuce cup with the watermelon salad using a spoon. f) Before serving, let the cups cool for five minutes. g) If desired, garnish with more basil leaves. h) For a cool bite, serve right away!

38. Tangy Pineapple Salsa with Baked Chips

Total Time: 20 minutes | Prep Time: 10 minutes

Ingredients:

- 1 cup fresh pineapple chunks
- 1/4 cup red onion, chopped
- 1/2 teaspoon chilli powder
- 4 small whole wheat tortillas, cut into triangles
- 1/2 cup diced red bell pepper
- 1 tablespoon lime juice
- 1/4 teaspoon salt

Directions:

a) Set the oven's temperature to 175°C (350°F). b) Place the tortilla triangles in a single layer on a baking sheet, and then bake them for eight to ten minutes or until they reach the desired level of crispiness. c) Meanwhile, fill the Ninja Blast Max Blender with pineapple, lime juice, salt, and chilli powder. To chop the pineapple slightly, blend it for a few seconds. d) Move to a bowl and combine with the red onion and chopped bell pepper. e) Give the salsa five minutes to settle so the flavours can combine. f) Warm baked chips should be served alongside. g) If desired, garnish with fresh cilantro. h) Savour it as an appetizer or snack!

39. Strawberry Coconut Chia Pudding

Total Time: 4 hours | Prep Time: 10 minutes

Ingredients:

- 1 cup coconut milk
- 2 tablespoons chia seeds
- 1/2 teaspoon vanilla extract
- 1/2 cup fresh strawberries
- 1 tablespoon maple syrup

Directions:

a) Add coconut milk, strawberries, maple syrup, and vanilla to the Ninja Blast Max Blender. Blend until it's smooth. b) Transfer the blend into a basin. c) Mix in the chia seeds until they are completely incorporated. d) Let sit for 5 minutes, then stir again to prevent clumping. e) For at least four hours or overnight, cover and place in the refrigerator. f) Before serving, stir once more once it has set. g) Add some coconut flakes or fresh strawberries as a garnish. h) Enjoy chilled as a nutritious breakfast or snack!

40. Mango Pineapple Salsa with Cinnamon Chips

Total Time: 15 minutes | Prep Time: 15 minutes

Ingredients:

1 cup fresh mango, diced	1 cup fresh pineapple, diced
¼ cup red bell pepper, diced	¼ cup red onion, diced
1 tablespoon fresh cilantro, chopped	1 tablespoon lime juice
½ teaspoon salt	½ teaspoon honey (optional)
4 small flour tortillas	1 tablespoon melted butter
1 teaspoon cinnamon sugar	

Directions:

a) Set the oven's temperature to 175°C (350°F). b) Sprinkle the flour tortillas with cinnamon sugar after brushing them with melted butter. Slice into triangles. c) Place the pieces of tortilla on a baking sheet and bake for 8 to 10 minutes or until they are crispy. Let it cool. d) Add the mango, pineapple, red bell pepper, red onion, cilantro, lime juice, salt, and honey to the Ninja Blast Max Blender. e) Until the ingredients are thoroughly blended but still have some chunks, pulse the blender a few times. f) To allow the flavours to meld, move the salsa to a serving dish and let it be there for a few minutes. g) Enjoy with cinnamon chips on the side!

41. Chocolate Almond Date Energy Bites

Total Time: 15 minutes | Prep Time: 15 minutes

Ingredients:

1 cup pitted Medjool dates	½ cup almonds
¼ cup unsweetened cocoa powder	1 teaspoon vanilla extract
¼ teaspoon sea salt	1 tablespoon chia seeds
2 tablespoons shredded coconut (optional)	

Directions:

a) After five minutes of softening in warm water, drain the dates. b) Pulse the almonds in the Ninja Blast Max Blender until they are finely chopped. c) Add the sea salt, chia seeds, dates, cocoa powder, and vanilla essence. Blend until the mixture has the consistency of thick dough. d) Blend again after adding one teaspoon of water at a time if the mixture is too dry. e) One spoonful of the ingredients should be scooped out and rolled into a ball. f) You may choose to wrap each energy snack with coconut shreds. g) To firm up, place the bits on a platter and place them in the refrigerator for 15 minutes. h) Keep in the refrigerator for up to a week in an airtight container.

42. Creamy Peanut Butter Apple Dip

Total Time: 5 minutes | Prep Time: 5 minutes

Ingredients:

½ cup Greek yogurt	¼ cup creamy peanut butter
1 tablespoon honey	½ teaspoon cinnamon
1 teaspoon vanilla extract	1 tablespoon chopped peanuts (optional)
Sliced apples for dipping	

Directions:

a) Add Greek yoghurt, peanut butter, honey, cinnamon, and vanilla extract to the Ninja Blast Max Blender. b) Blend till creamy and smooth. c) To guarantee uniform mixing, scrape down the sides as necessary. d) Move to a small bowl and, if using, top with chopped peanuts. e) Serve with sliced apples right away. f) You may keep leftovers in the refrigerator for up to three days.

43. Raspberry Lemon Cheesecake Dip

Total Time: 10 minutes | Prep Time: 10 minutes

Ingredients:

- ½ cup cream cheese, softened
- ½ cup Greek yogurt
- 2 tablespoons honey
- 1 teaspoon lemon zest
- 1 tablespoon lemon juice
- ½ cup fresh raspberries
- Graham crackers or fruit for dipping

Directions:

a) Cream cheese, Greek yoghurt, honey, lemon zest, and lemon juice should all be added to the Ninja Blast Max Blender. b) Blend till creamy and smooth. c) Pulse a few times to incorporate the raspberries, leaving them somewhat chunky. d) To thoroughly combine everything, scrape down the sides as necessary. e) Move to a bowl for serving. f) If you want to dip anything, serve it with fresh fruit or graham crackers.

BREAKFAST RECIPES

44. Banana Almond Power Smoothie

Total Time: 5 minutes | Prep Time: 5 minutes

Ingredients:

- 1 banana
- 1 cup unsweetened almond milk
- 1 tablespoon almond butter
- 1 tablespoon flaxseeds
- ½ teaspoon cinnamon
- 1 teaspoon honey (optional)
- ½ cup ice cubes

Directions:

a) Slice and peel the banana. b) Add banana, almond milk, almond butter, flaxseeds, cinnamon, honey, and ice cubes to the Ninja Blast Max Blender. c) Blend till creamy and smooth. d) Increase the amount of almond milk and mix again if the smoothie is too thick. e) Pour into a glass and start drinking right away.

45. Classic Strawberry Banana Shake

Total Time: 5 minute | Prep Time: 5 minutes

Ingredients:

- 1 cup frozen strawberries
- 1 ripe banana
- 1/2 cup milk (dairy or non-dairy)
- 1/2 cup Greek yogurt
- 1 tsp honey or sweetener (optional)
- Ice cubes (optional)

Directions:

a) Put the banana and frozen strawberries in the Ninja Blast Max blender. b) Pour in the Greek yoghurt and milk. c) If desired, drizzle with honey or sweetener. d) For a thicker texture, feel free to add a handful of ice cubes. e) Put the cover on tightly and mix for 30 to 60 seconds at high speed. f) Serve the shake right away after pouring it into a glass.

46. Blueberry Oatmeal Smoothie

Total Time: 5 minutes | Prep Time: 5 minutes

Ingredients:

1/4 cup rolled oats	1 cup frozen blueberries
1/2 cup almond milk	1/2 banana
1/2 tsp cinnamon	1/4 cup Greek yogurt
	Ice cubes (optional)

Directions:

a) Put the banana, oats, and frozen blueberries in the blender. b) Add the Greek yoghurt and almond milk. c) For added taste, add some cinnamon. d) Add ice cubes for a thicker thickness. e) Blend until smooth, 30 to 60 seconds on high speed. f) If desired, use honey or another sweetener to modify the sweetness after tasting. g) Transfer to a glass and savour.

47. Peanut Butter Banana Protein Shake

Total Time: 5 minutes | Prep Time: 5 minutes

Ingredients:

2 tbsp peanut butter	1 ripe banana
	1 scoop protein powder (optional)
1/2 cup almond milk	1/4 cup Greek yogurt
Ice cubes (optional)	

Directions:

a) Put the protein powder, peanut butter, and banana in the blender. b) For creaminess, mix with Greek yoghurt and almond milk. c) If you want a thicker shake, you may optionally add ice cubes. d) Put the lid on and mix for 30 to 60 seconds on high. e) Pour into a glass once it's smooth. f) Savour your high-protein smoothie for breakfast or as a post-workout treat.

48. Mango Pineapple Sunrise Smoothie

Total Time: 5 minutes | Prep Time: 5 minutes

Ingredients:

1/2 cup frozen pineapple chunks	1/2 cup frozen mango chunks
1/4 cup coconut milk	1/2 cup orange juice
Ice cubes (optional)	1 tsp honey (optional)

Directions:

a) Put pieces of frozen pineapple and mango in the blender. b) Add the coconut milk and orange juice. c) If desired, add honey for sweetness. d) If you want the consistency to be more substantial, add a few ice cubes. e) Cover and mix for 30 to 60 seconds. f) When well combined, transfer to a glass. g) Serve right away for a cool, tropical beverage.

49. Green Detox Breakfast Smoothie

Total Time: 5 minutes | Prep Time: 5 minutes

Ingredients:

	1/2 cup spinach leaves
1/2 banana	1/2 apple (cored and chopped)
1/2 cup cucumber (chopped)	1/2 cup coconut water or water
1 tbsp chia seeds	Ice cubes (optional)

Directions:

a) Put the cucumber, apple, banana, and spinach in the blender. b) Add water to hydrate or coconut water. c) For an additional fibre boost, add chia seeds. d) If you want the smoothie to be cold, add some ice cubes. e) For 30 to 60 seconds, blend everything at high speed until it's smooth. f) If necessary, use honey or another sweetener to modify the sweetness based on taste. g) Enjoy the advantages of a green detox by pouring it into a glass and drinking it.

50. Chocolate Avocado Energy Shake

Total Time: 5 minutes | Prep Time: 5 minutes

Ingredients:

1 tablespoon cocoa powder

1 cup almond milk (or any milk of choice)

1 ripe avocado

1 tablespoon honey or maple syrup

1/2 teaspoon vanilla extract

Ice cubes (optional)

Directions:

a) After halving the avocado, remove the pit with a spoon. Add the meat to the blender after scooping it out. b) In the blender, combine the vanilla essence, honey or maple syrup, and cocoa powder. c) Add almond milk. d) For a thicker, colder shake, add a handful of ice cubes. e) On high, blend until creamy and smooth. f) If needed, add extra honey or syrup after tasting to regulate the sweetness. g) Transfer to a glass and serve right away.

51. Vanilla Chia Protein Shake

Total Time: 5 minutes | Prep Time: 5 minutes

Ingredients:

1 tablespoon chia seeds

1/2 banana

1 scoop vanilla protein powder

1 cup milk of choice

1/2 teaspoon vanilla extract

Ice cubes (optional)

Directions:

a) Put the banana, chia seeds, protein powder, and vanilla essence in the blender. b) To make the shake thicker, add the milk and ice cubes. c) On high, blend until all ingredients are smooth and properly blended. d) To enable the chia seeds to absorb liquid and thicken the shake, let the mixture rest for one minute. e) Blend once more if necessary to smooth up any leftover pieces. f) Transfer to a glass and immediately savour.

52. Creamy Coffee Breakfast Shake

Total Time: 5 minutes | Prep Time: 5 minutes

Ingredients:

1/2 cup milk of choice

1/2 frozen banana

1/2 cup brewed coffee (cooled)

1 tablespoon almond butter or peanut butter

1 tablespoon honey or sweetener of choice

Ice cubes (optional)

Directions:

a) Make a potent brew and allow it to cool to room temperature. b) In the blender, combine the milk, honey, frozen banana, almond butter, and cooled coffee. c) To make it thicker and colder, add ice cubes. d) On high, blend until everything is creamy and smooth. e) If necessary, add extra honey or sweetness after tasting. f) Enjoy your invigorating morning smoothie after pouring it into a glass!

53. Tropical Coconut Mango Shake

Total Time: 5 minutes | Prep Time: 5 minutes

Ingredients:

1/2 cup frozen pineapple chunks

1/4 cup Greek yogurt

1/2 cup frozen mango chunks

1/2 cup coconut milk (or milk of choice)

1 teaspoon honey or agave syrup

Ice cubes (optional)

Directions:

a) In the blender, combine Greek yoghurt, frozen pineapple, and frozen mango. b) Add honey and coconut milk. c) To create a frosted effect, add ice cubes. d) Using a high speed, blend until everything is smooth and creamy. e) If you want additional sweetness, taste and add more honey. f) Pour into a glass and savour the tastes of the tropics!

54. Apple Cinnamon Breakfast Smoothie

Total Time: 5 minutes | Prep Time: 5 minutes

Ingredients:

	1 medium apple, cored and chopped
1/2 cup rolled oats	1/2 teaspoon cinnamon
1/2 cup almond milk (or milk of choice)	1/4 cup Greek yogurt
1 tablespoon honey (optional)	Ice cubes (optional)

Directions:

a) In the blender, combine the Greek yoghurt, rolled oats, cinnamon, and diced apple. b) If using, add honey and almond milk. c) If you want your smoothie cooler, add ice cubes. d) On high, blend until creamy and smooth. e) If necessary, add additional honey after tasting to regulate the sweetness. f) Enjoy this nutritious, breakfast-ready smoothie after pouring it into a glass!

55. Spinach and Pineapple Morning Blend

Total Time: 5 minutes | Prep Time: 5 minutes

Ingredients:

1 cup fresh spinach

1 cup pineapple chunks (fresh or frozen)	1 banana
1/2 cup coconut water	1 tablespoon chia seeds (optional)
1/2 cup ice	

Directions:

a) In the blender, combine the banana, pineapple pieces, and spinach. b) Add chia seeds (optional) and coconut water. c) For a cooled texture, add ice. d) Cover and process on high until smooth. e) If necessary, add additional coconut water after checking the consistency. f) Transfer to a glass and serve right away.

56. Pumpkin Spice Smoothie

Total Time: 5 minutes | Prep Time: 5 minutes

Ingredients:

	1/2 cup pumpkin puree
1/2 cup almond milk (or milk of choice)	1/2 banana
1/2 teaspoon pumpkin spice	1 tablespoon maple syrup or honey
1/4 teaspoon cinnamon	1/2 cup ice

Directions:

a) In the blender, combine the banana, almond milk, and pumpkin puree. b) Add maple syrup, cinnamon, and pumpkin spice. c) To cool the smoothie, add the ice cubes. d) Cover and mix for 30 to 45 seconds on high. e) If desired, add extra maple syrup to taste and adjust sweetness. f) Transfer to a glass, garnish with a dash of cinnamon, and savour.

57. Raspberry Oatmeal Shake

Total Time: 5 minutes | Prep Time: 5 minutes

Ingredients:

- 1/4 cup rolled oats
- 1 tablespoon honey or agave syrup
- 1/2 cup ice
- 1/2 cup raspberries (fresh or frozen)
- 1 cup unsweetened almond milk
- 1/4 teaspoon vanilla extract

Directions:

a) In the blender, combine almond milk, oats, and raspberries. b) For sweetness and flavour, add honey and vanilla essence. c) Add ice cubes for a chilly, revitalizing feel. d) Cover and process on high until smooth. e) Increase the amount of almond milk and combine once more if the consistency is too thick. f) Transfer to a glass and serve right away.

58. Carrot Ginger Power Shake

Total Time: 5 minutes | Prep Time: 5 minutes

Ingredients:

- 1/2 inch piece of fresh ginger, peeled
- 1/2 cup Greek yoghurt (or dairy-free alternative)
- 1/2 cup ice
- 1 medium carrot, peeled and chopped
- 1/2 cup orange juice
- 1 tablespoon honey or maple syrup

Directions:

a) In the blender, combine the orange juice, diced carrot, and fresh ginger. b) For protein and creaminess, add Greek yoghurt. c) Use maple syrup or honey to sweeten. d) To cool and thicken the shake, add ice. e) Cover and process until creamy and smooth. f) Serve right away after tasting and adjusting the sweetness.

59. Chocolate Peanut Butter Breakfast Shake

Total Time: 5 minutes | Prep Time: 5 minutes

Ingredients:

- 1 tablespoon cocoa powder
- 1/2 cup almond milk (or milk of choice)
- 1 tablespoon honey or maple syrup
- 1 tablespoon peanut butter
- 1 banana
- 1/2 cup Greek yoghurt (or dairy-free alternative)
- 1/2 cup ice

Directions:

a) Put the banana, peanut butter, and chocolate powder in the blender. b) Add Greek yoghurt and almond milk for creaminess. c) Use maple syrup or honey to sweeten. d) For a chilly texture, add ice. e) Cover and mix for 30 to 45 seconds on high. f) Enjoy a rich, nutritious morning shake after pouring it into a glass.

60. Pear and Almond Milk Smoothie

Total Time: 5 minutes | Prep Time: 5 minutes

Ingredients:

- 1/2 cup unsweetened almond milk
- 1 tablespoon honey (optional)
- Ice cubes (optional)
- 1 pear, cored and chopped
- 1/2 cup Greek yogurt
- 1/4 teaspoon ground cinnamon

Directions:

a) In the Ninja Blast Max blender, combine the diced pear, Greek yoghurt, almond milk, honey, and cinnamon. b) In order to make your beverage colder, you need to add some ice cubes.

c) Put the cover on and mix until smooth, 30 seconds on high. d) If required, add extra honey after tasting to adjust sweetness. e) Pour a glass of the smoothie. f) If preferred, top with a dusting of cinnamon and serve right away.

61. Avocado and Matcha Protein Shake

Total Time: 5 minutes | Prep Time: 5 minutes

Ingredients:

	1 ripe avocado, peeled and pitted
1/2 cup almond milk	1 scoop vanilla protein powder
1 teaspoon matcha powder	1 tablespoon chia seeds
1 tablespoon honey (optional)	Ice cubes

Directions:

a) In the Ninja Blast Max blender, combine the avocado, almond milk, protein powder, matcha powder, chia seeds, and honey. b) For a thick, cold shake, add a few ice cubes. c) Blend until smooth and creamy, 30 to 45 seconds on high. d) If required, add extra honey after tasting to adjust sweetness. e) Fill a glass with the shake. f) Serve right now, and feel free to add some chia seeds on top.

62. Blackberry Banana Blast

Total Time: 5 minutes | Prep Time: 5 minutes

Ingredients:

	1 ripe banana
1/2 cup fresh blackberries	1/2 cup almond milk
1/4 cup Greek yogurt	1 tablespoon honey (optional)
Ice cubes	

Directions:

a) In the blender, combine the Greek yoghurt, honey, almond milk, banana, and blackberries. b) For a cooler, thicker texture, add ice cubes. c) Blend until smooth and creamy, 30 to 45 seconds on high. d) If necessary, taste and add honey for additional sweetness. e) Pour a glass of the smoothie. f) Savour the delicious taste explosion right away.

63. Strawberry Cheesecake Smoothie

Total Time: 5 minutes | Prep Time: 5 minutes

Ingredients:

	1 cup fresh strawberries, hulled
1/4 cup low-fat cream cheese	1/2 cup almond milk
1 tablespoon honey or maple syrup	1/2 teaspoon vanilla extract
1/4 cup crushed graham crackers (optional)	Ice cubes

Directions:

a) In the Ninja Blast Max blender, combine the almond milk, cream cheese, honey, vanilla essence, and strawberries. b) Add the crumbled graham crackers for a texture similar to cheesecake. c) To freeze and thicken the smoothie, add ice cubes. d) Blend till smooth and creamy, 30 seconds on high. e) If necessary, taste and adjust the sweetness. f) If desired, top with more crumbled graham crackers after pouring into a glass.

64. Pomegranate Berry Antioxidant Shake

Total Time: 5 minutes | Prep Time: 5 minutes

Ingredients:

	1/2 cup pomegranate seeds

1/2 cup mixed berries (blueberries, raspberries, or strawberries)	1/2 cup Greek yogurt
1 tablespoon flaxseeds	1 tablespoon honey (optional)
1/2 cup almond milk	Ice cubes

Directions:

a) In the blender, combine the almond milk, Greek yoghurt, flaxseeds, honey, mixed berries, and pomegranate seeds. b) For a thicker consistency and a cool beverage, add ice cubes. c) Blend until smooth, 30 to 45 seconds on high. d) If required, add extra honey after tasting to adjust sweetness. e) Transfer to a glass. f) Serve right away for an antioxidant boost!

65. Vanilla Pumpkin Pie Shake

Total Time: 5 minutes | Prep Time: 5 minutes

Ingredients:

	1 cup canned pumpkin
1 frozen banana	1 cup almond milk
1/2 tsp vanilla extract	1/2 tsp cinnamon
1/4 tsp nutmeg	1 tbsp honey (optional)

Directions:

a) Fill your Ninja Blast Max Blender with almond milk, canned pumpkin, frozen bananas, and vanilla extract. b) Add the nutmeg and cinnamon and stir. c) Optional: For a hint of sweetness, add honey. d) Cover and process on high until smooth. e) To get the correct consistency, add a small amount of almond milk if the shake is too thick. f) If preferred, top with a few pumpkin seeds or a dusting of cinnamon after pouring into a glass. g) Savour your rich, fall-themed smoothie!

66. Pineapple Coconut Chia Shake

Total Time: 5 minutes | Prep Time: 5 minutes

Ingredients:

	1 cup fresh or frozen pineapple chunks
1/2 cup coconut milk	1/4 cup coconut yoghurt
1 tbsp chia seeds	1/2 tbsp honey (optional)

Directions:

a) In the blender, combine the chia seeds, pineapple pieces, coconut milk, and coconut yoghurt. b) Add honey to your shake if you want it sweeter. c) On high, blend until creamy and smooth. d) Add extra coconut milk or a dash of water if the shake is too thick. e) To scatter the chia seeds, pour into a glass and give it a good swirl. f) Allowing it to sit for one minute will allow the chia seeds to absorb part of the liquid, which will result in a thicker consistency. g) Savour your refreshing, tropical smoothie!

67. Choco-Banana Nut Shake

Total Time: 5 minutes | Prep Time: 5 minutes

Ingredients:

	1 frozen banana
1 tbsp cocoa powder	1/2 cup almond milk
1 tbsp peanut butter or almond butter	1 tbsp honey or maple syrup
1/4 tsp vanilla extract	

Directions:

a) In the blender, combine the peanut butter, almond milk, chocolate powder, and frozen banana. b) For sweetness, add the honey or maple syrup. c) To add even more flavour, add the vanilla extract. d) Make sure all the ingredients are well blended and blend until smooth. e) If the shake is too thick, thin it up with a little more almond milk. f) Transfer into a glass and savour the rich, chocolaty flavour! g) If desired, add some chopped nuts as a garnish.

68. Creamy Cashew Date Smoothie

Total Time: 5 minutes | Prep Time: 5 minutes

Ingredients:

	1/4 cup raw cashews
2 dates, pitted	1 cup unsweetened almond milk
1/2 frozen banana	1/2 tsp vanilla extract

Directions:

a) For a smoother texture, soak cashews and dates in warm water for about five minutes. b) In the blender, combine the cashews that have been soaked, dates, frozen banana, almond milk, and vanilla essence. c) Using a high speed, blend until everything is smooth and creamy. d) Add a little honey or an additional date if you want a sweeter smoothie. e) Pour into a glass and savour the cashew and date's deep, nutty taste! f) For added crunch, you may also sprinkle some crushed cashews on top.

69. Orange Mango Energy Boost Smoothie

Total Time: 5 minutes | Prep Time: 5 minutes

Ingredients:

	1 orange, peeled
1/2 cup frozen mango chunks	1/2 cup spinach (optional)
1/2 cup coconut water	1 tbsp honey or agave syrup (optional)

Directions:

a) In the blender, combine the frozen mango, orange peel, and spinach if using. b) If desired, add sugar after adding the coconut water. c) For one to two minutes on high, blend until smooth and creamy. d) Add extra coconut water if the consistency is too thick. e) Enjoy the colourful, invigorating smoothie after pouring it into a glass. f) For an added refreshing touch, garnish with a slice of orange or some fresh mint leaves.

70. Raspberry Vanilla Yogurt Shake

Total Time: 5 minutes | Prep Time: 5 minutes

Ingredients:

	1 cup raspberries (fresh or frozen)
1/2 cup plain Greek yogurt	1/2 cup almond milk
1 tablespoon honey or maple syrup	1/2 teaspoon vanilla extract
Ice cubes (optional)	

Directions:

a) In the Ninja Blast Max blender, combine the almond milk, Greek yoghurt, raspberries, honey, and vanilla extract. b) For a thicker texture, add ice cubes. c) Cover and process on high until creamy and smooth. d) If necessary, taste and adjust the sweetness. e) Fill a glass with the shake. f) Add some fresh raspberries as a garnish. g) Serve right away and savour!

71. Apple Pie Smoothie

Total Time: 5 minutes | Prep Time: 5 minutes

Ingredients:

	1 medium apple, peeled, cored, and chopped
1/2 banana	1/2 teaspoon cinnamon
1/4 teaspoon ground nutmeg	1/2 cup unsweetened almond milk
1/4 cup oats	1 tablespoon maple syrup

Ice cubes

Directions:

a) In the blender, combine the apple, banana, oats, almond milk, cinnamon, nutmeg, and maple syrup. b) For a cooler smoothie, add ice cubes. c) Blend until smooth and creamy, approximately 30 seconds on high. d) Blend the smoothie again after adding a little more almond milk if it's too thick. e) Taste and adjust the spice or sweetness as necessary. f) Transfer to a glass and garnish with a bit more cinnamon. g) Enjoy the deliciousness of apple pie right now!

72. Coconut Matcha Latte Smoothie

Total Time: 5 minutes | Prep Time: 5 minutes

Ingredients:

	1 teaspoon matcha powder
1/2 cup coconut milk	1/2 banana
1 tablespoon honey or agave syrup	1/2 cup ice
1/2 teaspoon vanilla extract	

Directions:

a) In your Ninja Blast Max blender, combine the matcha powder, banana, coconut milk, honey, and vanilla essence. b) To create a frosted effect, add ice cubes. c) On high, blend until everything is smooth and well blended. d) Add extra honey to taste and adjust sweetness as needed. e) Pour a glass of the smoothie. f) Add some matcha powder or shredded coconut as a garnish. g) Enjoy the green, creamy richness right away after serving!

73. High-Protein Coffee Shake

Total Time: 5 minutes | Prep Time: 5 minutes

Ingredients:

	1 cup cold brewed coffee (or strong brewed coffee)
1 scoop vanilla protein powder	1/2 banana
1/4 cup unsweetened almond milk	1/2 teaspoon cinnamon
1 tablespoon almond butter	Ice cubes

Directions:

a) Fill the Ninja Blast Max blender with the cold brewed coffee. b) Add the banana, almond milk, almond butter, cinnamon, and vanilla protein powder. c) A couple of ice cubes should be added. d) On high, blend until creamy and smooth. e) If required, add more almond butter or taste and adjust the sweetness. f) Fill a glass with the shake. g) Serve right now, and enjoy the protein boost!

74. Sweet Potato Breakfast Shake

Total Time: 5 minutes | Prep Time: 5 minutes

Ingredients:

	1/2 cup cooked sweet potato (peeled and mashed)
1/2 banana	1/2 cup unsweetened almond milk
1 tablespoon peanut butter or almond butter	1/2 teaspoon cinnamon
1 tablespoon maple syrup	Ice cubes

Directions:

a) Blend together the sweet potato that has been cooked, the banana, the peanut butter, the almond milk, the cinnamon, and the maple syrup from the blender. b) For a cold shake, add ice cubes. c) On high, blend until creamy and smooth. d) If necessary, taste and adjust the sweetness. e) Blend again after adding a little more almond milk if it's too thick. f) Transfer to a glass and top with more peanut butter or a dusting of cinnamon. g) Enjoy a warm, satisfying breakfast shake right away!

75. Honey Almond Breakfast Shake

Total Time: 5 minutes | Prep Time: 5 minutes

Ingredients:

	1 cup almond milk (or any milk of your choice)
1/2 cup Greek yogurt	1 tablespoon honey
1/4 cup almonds (soaked overnight if preferred)	1/2 banana
1/2 teaspoon vanilla extract	Ice cubes (optional)

Directions:

a) In the blender, combine Greek yoghurt and almond milk. b) Add the banana, almonds, and honey. c) For added taste, add the vanilla essence. d) Process the ingredients on high speed until they become creamy and smooth. e) If you want a thicker, colder consistency, add ice cubes. f) Continue blending until the drink is foamy and the ice has been pulverized. g) If necessary, taste and add additional honey to adjust sweetness. h) Transfer to a glass and serve right away.

76. Chocolate Hazelnut Morning Blend

Total Time: 5 minutes | Prep Time: 5 minutes

Ingredients:

	1 cup unsweetened almond milk
1 tablespoon cocoa powder	2 tablespoons hazelnut butter
1 tablespoon honey or maple syrup	1/2 frozen banana
1/4 teaspoon vanilla extract	Ice cubes (optional)

Directions:

a) Fill the blender with the almond milk. b) Stir in hazelnut butter, chocolate powder, and honey or maple syrup for sweetness. c) Add the vanilla essence and frozen banana. d) On high, blend until smooth and thoroughly mixed. e) If you want the mixture to be more thick, you may add ice cubes to it. f) Continue blending until the ice has been broken up and everything is smooth. g) To suit your preferences, taste and adjust the sweetness. h) Pour into a glass and start drinking right away.

77. Greek Yogurt and Honey Smoothie

Total Time: 5 minutes | Prep Time: 5 minutes

Ingredients:

	1 cup plain Greek yogurt
1 tablespoon honey	1/2 cup frozen mixed berries
1/4 cup water or coconut water	1/4 teaspoon vanilla extract
Ice cubes (optional)	

Directions:

a) In the blender, combine the Greek yoghurt and honey. b) Add water or coconut water and frozen mixed berries. c) For added taste, add vanilla extract. d) On high, blend until creamy and smooth. e) Add ice cubes for a thicker consistency. f) Blend one more until frothy and smooth. g) Taste and add additional honey if necessary to adjust sweetness. h) Enjoy right away after serving chilled in a glass.

78. Caramel Macchiato Protein Shake

Total Time: 5 minutes | Prep Time: 5 minutes

Ingredients:

- 1 cup unsweetened almond milk (or milk of choice)
- 1 scoop vanilla protein powder
- 1 tablespoon caramel sauce
- 1/2 cup cold brewed coffee
- 1/2 banana
- Ice cubes (optional)

Directions:

a) Fill the blender with the cold brewed coffee and almond milk. b) Add the banana, caramel sauce, and protein powder. c) On high, blend until the mixture is creamy and smooth. d) If you want a thicker, colder texture, add ice cubes. e) Blend one more until frothy and smooth. f) If desired, add extra caramel sauce after tasting to regulate the sweetness. g) Enjoy the rich, caffeinated shake after pouring it into a glass. h) If preferred, top with a drizzle of caramel sauce.

79. Maple Walnut Oatmeal Smoothie

Total Time: 5 minutes | Prep Time: 5 minutes

Ingredients:

- 1/2 cup rolled oats
- 1 cup unsweetened almond milk
- 1/4 cup walnuts (chopped)
- 1 tablespoon maple syrup
- 1/2 banana
- 1/4 teaspoon cinnamon
- Ice cubes (optional)

Directions:

a) In the blender, combine the almond milk and rolled oats. b) Add the banana, walnuts, and maple syrup. c) For added warmth, sprinkle in the cinnamon. d) On high, blend until smooth and thoroughly mixed. e) Add a handful of ice cubes for a thicker thickness. f) Repeatedly blend until well combined and foamy. g) You may alter the sweetness by adding more maple syrup to taste if you so choose. h) Enjoy a tasty and nutritious smoothie after pouring it into a glass.

80. Dark Chocolate Berry Shake

Total Time: 5 minutes | Prep Time: 5 minutes

Ingredients:

- 1 cup mixed berries (strawberries, blueberries, raspberries)
- 1 banana
- 1 tablespoon dark cocoa powder
- 1 cup milk (dairy or non-dairy)
- 1 tablespoon honey or sweetener of choice
- Ice cubes (optional)

Directions:

a) Put the banana and mixed berries in the Ninja Blast Max Blender. b) Add your preferred sweetener, milk, and cocoa powder. c) Blend until smooth, 30 to 60 seconds on high. d) If desired, add ice cubes and combine one more to get a cold, creamy shake. e) If additional honey is needed, taste and adjust the sweetness. f) Transfer to a glass and serve right away. g) Savour your chocolaty, fruity, and creamy shake!

81. Watermelon Mint Cooler

Total Time: 5 minutes | Prep Time: 5 minutes

Ingredients:

- 2 cups cubed watermelon
- 1/2 cup fresh mint leaves
- 1 tablespoon lime juice

1 teaspoon honey or agave syrup (optional)

1 cup cold water or coconut water

Ice cubes

Directions:

a) Put the mint leaves and watermelon cubes in the blender. b) Add the honey (if using) and lime juice. c) Pour in the coconut water or cold water. d) Blend until smooth, 30 to 60 seconds on high. e) As desired, alter the sweetness or mint taste by tasting it. f) Blend in ice cubes until cold. g) For a refreshing touch, pour into glasses and top with additional lime slices or a mint sprig. h) Serve right away and enjoy the refreshing beverage!

82. Coconut Vanilla Shake

Total Time: 5 minutes | Prep Time: 5 minutes

Ingredients:

1/2 cup Greek yoghurt or dairy-free yoghurt

1 cup coconut milk

1 teaspoon vanilla extract

1 tablespoon honey or sweetener of choice

Ice cubes

Directions:

a) Fill the Ninja Blast Max Blender with Greek yoghurt and coconut milk. b) Add the honey and vanilla extract. c) Blend the ingredients together on high for thirty to sixty seconds or until they reach a silky smooth and creamy consistency. d) Taste and adjust the vanilla taste or sweetness as needed. e) Blend in ice cubes until cold and thick. f) If desired, top with shredded coconut or a vanilla bean after pouring into a glass. g) Savour the tastes of the tropics and serve right away!

83. Cinnamon Roll Smoothie

Total Time: 5 minutes | Prep Time: 5 minutes

Ingredients:

1 frozen banana

1/2 cup rolled oats

1/2 teaspoon ground cinnamon

1 tablespoon maple syrup or honey

1 cup almond milk or milk of choice

Ice cubes

Directions:

a) Put the rolled oats and frozen banana in the blender. b) Pour in the maple syrup and sprinkle with the ground cinnamon. c) Add your favourite milk or almond milk. d) In a blender, blend the ingredients for thirty to sixty seconds on high speed until they are completely smooth and creamy. e) If necessary, add additional cinnamon or maple syrup after tasting to balance the sweetness. f) To make it thicker and colder, add ice cubes and combine once more. g) Transfer to a glass and serve right away. h) Savour the comforting smoothie with a hint of cinnamon!

84. Chia Berry Protein Shake

Total Time: 5 minutes | Prep Time: 5 minutes

Ingredients:

1 tablespoon chia seeds

1 cup mixed berries (fresh or frozen)

1/2 cup protein powder (vanilla or berry flavour)

1 cup almond milk or milk of choice

1 teaspoon honey or sweetener of choice

Ice cubes

Directions:

a) In the blender, combine the protein powder, chia seeds, and mixed berries. b) Add the honey and almond milk. c) To get a creamy and smooth consistency, blend the shake on high for thirty to sixty seconds or until it achieves the desired consistency. d) If necessary, add additional honey or sweetener after tasting and adjusting the sweetness. e) For a colder, thicker consistency, add ice cubes and mix once more. f) If you want a thicker shake, let the chia seeds soak in liquid for a minute. g) Transfer to a glass and serve right away. h) Savour the protein-rich and invigorating smoothie!

85. Mocha Almond Butter Shake

Total Time: 5 minutes | Prep Time: 5 minutes

Ingredients:

- 1 tablespoon almond butter
- 1/2 cup brewed coffee (cooled)
- 1 teaspoon honey (optional)
- 1 cup almond milk (unsweetened)
- 1 tablespoon cocoa powder
- 1 frozen banana
- Ice cubes (optional)

Directions:

a) In the blender, combine the brewed coffee, chocolate powder, almond milk, and almond butter. b) Add the honey (if used) and the frozen banana. c) Process on high speed until creamy and smooth. d) If required, add extra honey after tasting to adjust sweetness. e) For a thicker, colder texture, add ice cubes and mix once more. f) Transfer to a glass and serve right away.

86. Papaya Ginger Morning Drink

Total Time: 5 minutes | Prep Time: 5 minutes

Ingredients:

- 1/2 inch piece of fresh ginger (peeled)
- 1/2 cup coconut water
- 1 cup papaya (peeled and cubed)
- 1 tablespoon honey or agave
- 1/2 cup ice cubes

Directions:

a) In the blender, combine the papaya, honey, and fresh ginger. b) Add ice cubes and coconut water. c) Blend till creamy and smooth. d) If necessary, taste and adjust the sweetness. e) After pouring into a glass, enjoy your revitalizing morning beverage!

87. Banana Date Smoothie

Total Time: 5 minutes | Prep Time: 5 minutes

Ingredients:

- 4-5 pitted dates
- 1 tablespoon almond butter
- Ice cubes (optional)
- 1 ripe banana
- 1 cup almond milk
- 1/2 teaspoon ground cinnamon

Directions:

a) In the blender, combine the banana, dates, almond butter, almond milk, and cinnamon. b) If you want a thicker texture, add ice cubes. c) Blend until smooth and creamy. d) If necessary, add more dates to taste and adjust the sweetness. e) Transfer to a glass and savour!

88. Green Apple Kale Smoothie

Total Time: 5 minutes | Prep Time: 5 minutes

Ingredients:

- 1/2 cup kale leaves (stems removed)
- 1/2 cup water or coconut water
- Ice cubes (optional)
- 1 green apple (cored and chopped)
- 1/2 banana
- 1 tablespoon chia seeds (optional)

Directions:

a) Put the banana, kale leaves, and diced green apple in the blender. b) Add water or coconut water, and if you like, chia seeds. c) On high, blend until creamy and smooth. d) Include ice cubes in your smoothie if you want it to be thicker and frostier. e) If the smoothie is too thick, taste it and add extra water. f) Transfer to a glass and serve right away.

89. Cucumber Melon Refreshing Shake

Total Time: 5 minutes | Prep Time: 5 minutes

Ingredients:

	1/2 cucumber (peeled and chopped)
1 cup melon	1/2 cup coconut water
1 tablespoon lime juice	1 teaspoon honey (optional)
Ice cubes (optional)	

Directions:

a) Put the coconut water, melon, and cucumber in the blender. b) Honey and lime juice may be drizzled over the top for sweetness if preferred. c) Blend until it's smooth and revitalizing. d) If you want your shake colder, add ice cubes. e) If necessary, taste and add additional honey to adjust sweetness. f) Enjoy your cool shake after pouring it into a glass!

90. Chocolate Cherry Almond Shake

Total Time: 5 minutes | Prep Time: 5 minutes

Ingredients:

	1 cup almond milk
½ cup frozen cherries	2 tablespoons almond butter
1 tablespoon cocoa powder	1 tablespoon honey or maple syrup
½ teaspoon vanilla extract	Ice cubes (optional)

Directions:

a) Fill the Ninja Blast Max Blender with the almond milk. b) Add almond butter, cocoa powder, honey, vanilla essence, and frozen cherries. c) Blend on high for 30 to 60 seconds or until smooth and creamy. d) Add a few ice cubes and combine once more if you want your shake to be thicker. e) If desired, add extra honey or syrup to taste and adjust sweetness. f) Transfer to a glass and serve right away.

91. Vanilla Macadamia Shake

Total Time: 5 minutes | Prep Time: 5 minutes

Ingredients:

	1 cup almond milk or coconut milk
½ cup unsalted macadamia nuts	1 tablespoon honey or maple syrup
1 teaspoon vanilla extract	1 frozen banana
Ice cubes (optional)	

Directions:

a) Fill the blender with almond or coconut milk. b) Add the frozen banana, honey, macadamia nuts, and vanilla essence. c) Blend until smooth and creamy, 30 to 60 seconds on high. d) Add ice cubes and combine once more if you like a thicker thickness. e) If needed, adjust the sweetness by tasting it. f) Transfer into a glass, add crushed macadamia nuts as a garnish (if desired), and serve.

92. Strawberry Oatmeal Shake

Total Time: 5 minutes | Prep Time: 5 minutes

Ingredients:

	1 cup oat milk or regular milk
½ cup rolled oats	1 cup frozen strawberries

1 tablespoon honey or maple syrup	½ teaspoon cinnamon
1 teaspoon chia seeds	Ice cubes (optional)

Directions:

a) Fill the blender with ordinary milk or oat milk. b) Stir in chia seeds, honey, cinnamon, frozen strawberries, and rolled oats. c) Blend the ingredients together on high for thirty to sixty seconds or until the mixture is smooth and creamy. d) Add ice cubes and combine once more if you like a thicker shake. e) If you want it sweeter, taste it and add extra honey or syrup. f) For a cool treat, pour into a glass and serve right away.

93. Lemon Blueberry Morning Bliss

Total Time: 5 minutes | Prep Time: 5 minutes

Ingredients:

	1 cup water or coconut water
1 cup frozen blueberries	½ cup plain Greek yogurt
1 tablespoon honey or agave syrup	1 teaspoon lemon zest
1 tablespoon fresh lemon juice	Ice cubes (optional)

Directions:

a) Fill the blender with water (or coconut water). b) Stir in Greek yoghurt, honey, lemon zest, frozen blueberries, and fresh lemon juice. c) Blend on high for thirty to sixty seconds or until the mixture is completely smooth. d) Add ice cubes and combine once more to make the shake thicker. e) Adjust the sweetness by tasting and adding additional syrup or honey. f) Transfer to a glass, top with more blueberries if desired, and serve.

94. Choco-Coconut Power Shake

Total Time: 5 minutes | Prep Time: 5 minutes

Ingredients:

	1 cup coconut milk
1 tablespoon cocoa powder	1 tablespoon almond butter
1 tablespoon honey or maple syrup	1 frozen banana
½ teaspoon vanilla extract	Ice cubes (optional)

Directions:

a) Fill the Ninja Blast Max Blender with coconut milk. b) Add the frozen banana, honey, almond butter, cocoa powder, and vanilla extract. c) The mixture should be blended on high for thirty to sixty seconds or until it reaches a creamy and smooth consistency. d) Add ice cubes and combine once more if you like a colder shake. e) When you have tasted it, add more honey or syrup if you would want it to be sweeter. f) Transfer to a glass and savour!

LUNCH RECIPES

95. Nutty Banana Honey Smoothie

Total Time: 5 minutes | Prep Time: 5 minutes

Ingredients:

1 ripe banana	1 tablespoon peanut butter
1 tablespoon honey	1/2 cup milk
1/4 cup Greek yoghurt (optional for creaminess)	A pinch of cinnamon (optional)
Ice cubes (optional)	

Directions:

a) Break the banana into pieces after peeling it. Add it to your Ninja Blast Max Blender. b) In the blender, combine the milk, peanut butter, and honey. c) To make the smoothie creamier, add the Greek yoghurt now if using. d) In order to enhance the flavour of the combination, add a little bit of cinnamon. e) If you want your smoothie to be more refreshing and thicker, you could add some ice cubes to it. f) Put your blender's lid on and mix on high for 30 to 45 seconds or until smooth. g) Transfer to a glass and savour! For added sweetness, you might want to sprinkle a little extra honey on top.

96. Creamy Avocado Spinach Soup

Total Time: 25 minutes | Prep Time: 10 minutes

Ingredients:

	1 ripe avocado
2 cups fresh spinach leaves	1 cup vegetable broth
1/2 cup coconut milk	1 small onion, chopped
1 garlic clove, minced	Salt and pepper to taste
1 tbsp olive oil	

Directions:

a) Melt the olive oil in a saucepan by heating it over a medium flame. Sauté the chopped onion and garlic for around three minutes or until they are tender and aromatic. b) Add the avocado, coconut milk, spinach, vegetable broth, sautéed onion and garlic, and Ninja Blast Max Blender. c) Blend till creamy and smooth. If necessary, add extra broth to get a thinner consistency. d) To taste, add salt and pepper. e) Cook the soup for five minutes over medium heat, stirring it often, after pouring it into a saucepan. f) When well heated, transfer to bowls and serve warm.

97. Roasted Red Pepper & Tomato Soup

Total Time: 40 minutes | Prep Time: 15 minutes

Ingredients:

	2 red bell peppers, roasted and peeled
2 large tomatoes, chopped	1 small onion, chopped
2 garlic cloves, minced	2 cups vegetable broth
1/2 tsp smoked paprika	Salt and pepper to taste
1 tbsp olive oil	

Directions:

a) Set the oven's temperature to 400°F or 200°C. To get a browned appearance, roast the bell peppers on a baking sheet for around twenty minutes. After allowing them to cool, remove the skin. b) Bring the olive oil to a temperature that is somewhere between low and medium in a saucepan. Cook the garlic and onion for around four minutes or until they are tender. c) Add the roasted red peppers, tomatoes, sautéed onion, garlic, smoked paprika, and vegetable broth to the Ninja Blast Max Blender. d) On high, blend until creamy and smooth. e) After pouring the soup into a saucepan, cook it on medium for five to seven minutes, stirring now and again. f) Before serving hot, season to taste with salt and pepper.

98. Classic Green Detox Smoothie

Total Time: 5 minutes | Prep Time: 5 minutes

Ingredients:

	1/2 cup spinach leaves
1/2 cup cucumber, chopped	1/2 green apple, chopped

1/2 banana

1 cup water or coconut water

1 tbsp chia seeds

Ice cubes (optional)

Directions:

a) Fill the Ninja Blast Max Blender with spinach, cucumber, apple, banana, and chia seeds. b) If desired, add ice cubes after adding water or coconut water to the blender. c) Blend till creamy and smooth. d) If you want a thinner consistency, taste and add more water. e) Pour into a glass and start drinking right away!

99. Mango Pineapple Protein Shake

Total Time: 5 minutes | Prep Time: 5 minutes

Ingredients:

1/2 cup frozen pineapple chunks

1/2 cup coconut milk

1 tbsp honey (optional)

1 cup frozen mango chunks

1 scoop vanilla protein powder

1/2 cup water

Directions:

a) Fill the Ninja Blast Max Blender with frozen mango, pineapple, protein powder, coconut milk, and water. b) On high, blend until creamy and smooth. c) To add sweetness, taste, and honey, mix again to integrate. d) Transfer to a glass and serve cold.

100. Strawberry Banana Oatmeal Smoothie

Total Time: 5 minutes | Prep Time: 5 minutes

Ingredients:

1/2 banana

1/2 cup strawberries (fresh or frozen)

1/4 cup rolled oats

1/2 cup almond milk (or any milk of choice)

1/2 tsp vanilla extract

Ice cubes (optional)

Directions:

a) In the Ninja Blast Max Blender, combine the banana, rolled oats, almond milk, vanilla extract, and strawberries. b) For a cooled smoothie, you may optionally add ice cubes. c) In order to get the appropriate consistency, if more milk is required, combine the ingredients until they are smooth and creamy. d) Pour into a glass and start drinking right away.

101. Creamy Peanut Butter Banana Shake

Total Time: 5 minutes | Prep Time: 5 minutes

Ingredients:

2 tbsp peanut butter

1 tsp honey (optional)

4-6 ice cubes

1 ripe banana

1 cup almond milk

1/2 tsp vanilla extract

Directions:

a) Break the banana into pieces after peeling it. b) In the blender, combine the banana, peanut butter, almond milk, honey, and vanilla extract. c) Add the ice cubes to get a cold consistency. d) On high, blend until creamy and smooth. e) Blend the smoothie again after adding a little more almond milk if it's too thick. f) Pour into a glass and start drinking right away.

102. Iced Mocha Protein Shake

Total Time: 5 minutes | Prep Time: 5 minutes

Ingredients:

1/2 cup brewed coffee (cooled)

- 1 scoop of chocolate protein powder
- 1 tbsp cocoa powder
- 1/2 cup almond milk
- 1/2 tsp vanilla extract
- 4-6 ice cubes

Directions:

a) Make a cup of coffee, then let it cool. b) Pour the chilled coffee, almond milk, chocolate protein powder, cocoa powder, and vanilla extract into the blender. c) To get a frosty finish, add ice cubes to the mixer. d) Blend the ingredients until it's frothy and smooth. e) If necessary, add a little amount of sweetness (such as honey or stevia) after tasting. f) For an added treat, top it with chocolate shavings or whipped cream after pouring it into a tall glass.

103. Vegan Chocolate Almond Smoothie

Total Time: 5 minutes | Prep Time: 5 minutes

Ingredients:

- 1/2 cup frozen banana slices
- 2 tbsp cacao powder
- 1/2 tsp cinnamon
- 1/2 cup almond milk
- 2 tbsp almond butter
- 1 tbsp maple syrup
- 1/2 tsp vanilla extract
- 4-6 ice cubes

Directions:

a) Almond milk, frozen banana slices, almond butter, cacao powder, maple syrup, cinnamon, and vanilla extract should all be combined in your blender. b) For a chilly, silky texture, add ice cubes. c) On high, blend until everything is creamy and well combined. d) If the consistency is too thick, thin it up with additional almond milk. e) Transfer into a glass and sprinkle with cinnamon or cacao powder for decoration. f) Serve this luscious vegan smoothie right now, and savour it!

104. Spiced Pumpkin Pie Smoothie

Total Time: 5 minutes | Prep Time: 5 minutes

Ingredients:

- 1/2 cup almond milk
- 1 tsp pumpkin pie spice
- 1/4 tsp ground ginger
- 4-6 ice cubes
- 1/2 cup canned pumpkin puree
- 1/2 frozen banana
- 1 tbsp maple syrup
- 1/4 tsp cinnamon

Directions:

a) Fill the blender with the pureed pumpkin. b) Add the ground ginger, cinnamon, maple syrup, pumpkin pie spice, almond milk, and frozen banana. c) To cool the smoothie, add the ice cubes. d) Adjust with more almond milk if necessary, and blend until smooth and creamy. e) You may alter the sweetness by adding more maple syrup to taste if you so choose. f) A dollop of whipped cream or a sprinkling of cinnamon may be used as a garnish; the mixture should be poured into a glass and served as quickly as feasible.

105. Green Goddess Gazpacho

Total Time: 10 minutes | Prep Time: 10 minutes

Ingredients:

- 1/2 avocado
- 1/2 cup parsley
- 1/4 cup lime juice
- 1 garlic clove, minced
- 1 cup cucumber, peeled and chopped
- 1/2 cup spinach leaves
- 1/4 cup olive oil
- 1/2 cup water (or as needed)
- 1/2 tsp salt

1/4 tsp pepper	4-6 ice cubes

Directions:

a) In a blender, combine the avocado, cucumber, spinach, parsley, garlic, lime juice, olive oil, and salt & pepper. Blend until the ingredients are smooth. b) Pour in the water and process until the mixture is completely pureed. c) Add additional water and combine once more to get a thinner consistency. d) Proceed with the processing until the mixture is fully smooth and frozen. e) If more salt or lime juice is required, it should be added after the seasoning has been tasted and adjusted. f) Transfer to glasses or bowls and sprinkle with cucumber slices or more parsley. Serve right away.

106. Butternut Squash & Carrot Soup

Total Time: 30 minutes | Prep Time: 10 minutes

Ingredients:

	2 cups butternut squash, peeled and cubed
1 cup carrots, peeled and sliced	1 medium onion, chopped
2 cloves garlic, minced	4 cups vegetable broth
1/2 teaspoon ground cumin	1/4 teaspoon ground cinnamon
Salt and pepper to taste	1 tablespoon olive oil

Directions:

a) In a blender, combine the avocado, cucumber, spinach, parsley, garlic, lime juice, olive oil, and salt & pepper. Blend until the ingredients are smooth. b) Pour in the water and process until the mixture is completely pureed. c) Add additional water and combine once more to get a thinner consistency. d) Add ice cubes and process until smooth and frozen. e) If necessary, add more salt or lime juice after tasting and adjusting the seasoning. f) Transfer to glasses or bowls and sprinkle with cucumber slices or more parsley. Serve right away.

107. Tropical Mango Coconut Smoothie

Total Time: 5 minutes | Prep Time: 5 minutes

Ingredients:

	1 cup frozen mango chunks
1/2 cup coconut milk	1/2 cup pineapple chunks
1/2 banana	1 tablespoon honey (optional)
Ice cubes (optional)	

Directions:

a) In the blender, combine the banana, pineapple, mango, coconut milk, and honey if using. b) By adding ice cubes and blending on high until smooth, you may get a thicker consistency in your beverage. c) If you want additional sweetness, taste and add more honey. d) Transfer the smoothie into glasses and add a pineapple or banana slice as a garnish. e) Savour the tastes of the tropics and serve right away!

108. Creamy Sweet Corn Soup

Total Time: 25 minutes | Prep Time: 10 minutes

Ingredients:

	2 cups corn kernels (fresh or frozen)
1 medium onion, chopped	2 cloves garlic, minced
3 cups vegetable broth	1/2 cup coconut cream or heavy cream
Salt and pepper to taste	1 tablespoon olive oil

Directions:

a) In a saucepan, heat the olive oil over medium heat. Sauté the garlic and onion for around three minutes or until they are tender. b) Immediately after adding the corn kernels and vegetable broth to the pot, bring the mixture to a boil. c) Cook the corn for 10 minutes, or until it reaches the desired level of tenderness, after reducing the heat to a simmer. d) Blend the mixture until it is smooth after transferring it to the Ninja Blast Max blender. e) Following the addition of the coconut cream, the soup should be seasoned with salt and pepper before being returned to the stove. f) Before serving, let it heat through for a further two to three minutes.

109. Mediterranean Hummus Dip

Total Time: 10 minutes | Prep Time: 10 minutes

Ingredients:

	1 can (15 oz) chickpeas, drained
2 tablespoons tahini	1 tablespoon olive oil
2 tablespoons lemon juice	1 garlic clove
1/2 teaspoon ground cumin	Salt and pepper to taste
Paprika (for garnish)	

Directions:

a) In the blender, combine the chickpeas, tahini, lemon juice, olive oil, cumin, garlic, salt, and pepper. b) If needed, scrape down the edges of the blender as you blend until smooth. c) If necessary, add extra salt or lemon juice after tasting and adjusting the seasoning. d) Pour a little more olive oil over it after transferring it to a serving dish. e) Sprinkle some paprika on top as a garnish. f) Serve with crackers, pita bread, or veggie sticks.

110. Spicy Black Bean Soup

Total Time: 30 minutes | Prep Time: 10 minutes

Ingredients:

	2 cups cooked black beans
1 medium onion, chopped	1 red bell pepper, chopped
2 cloves garlic, minced	2 cups vegetable broth
1/2 teaspoon chilli powder	1/4 teaspoon cayenne pepper
Salt and pepper to taste	1 tablespoon olive oil

Directions:

a) In a saucepan, heat the olive oil over medium heat. Sauté the bell pepper, garlic, and onion for 3-4 minutes or until they are tender. b) Add the cayenne, chilli powder, black beans, vegetable broth, salt, and pepper. c) After bringing the soup to a boil, lower the heat and simmer it for ten to fifteen minutes. d) Blend until smooth after transferring half of the soup to the Ninja Blast Max blender. e) Transfer the mixture that has been blended back into the pot, and then stir everything together. f) If necessary, reheat the soup for a few more minutes and adjust the spices to taste. g) If preferred, top with a dollop of sour cream or cilantro and serve hot.

111. Zesty Cilantro Lime Dressing

Total Time: 5 minutes | Prep Time: 5 minutes

Ingredients:

	1 cup fresh cilantro leaves
1/4 cup olive oil	2 tablespoons lime juice
1 tablespoon honey or agave syrup	1/2 teaspoon garlic powder
1/4 teaspoon salt	1/4 teaspoon black pepper

Directions:

a) In your Ninja Blast Max blender, combine the cilantro, olive oil, lime juice, honey, garlic powder, salt, and pepper. b) Blend until smooth and creamy, 30 to 45 seconds on high speed. c) If necessary, add extra salt or lime juice after tasting and adjusting the seasoning. d) Transfer to a bottle or jar. e) You may keep it in the fridge for up to a week. f) Before serving, give it a good shake.

112. Creamy Avocado Dressing

Total Time: 10 minutes | Prep Time: 10 minutes

Ingredients:

	1 ripe avocado, peeled and pitted
1/4 cup plain Greek yogurt	2 tablespoons lime juice
1 tablespoon olive oil	1 garlic clove, minced
1/4 teaspoon cumin	Salt and pepper, to taste

Directions:

a) In your Ninja Blast Max blender, combine the avocado, Greek yoghurt, lime juice, olive oil, cumin, and garlic. b) Blend until smooth, 30–40 seconds on high speed. c) Season with salt and pepper according to taste. d) If necessary, alter the consistency by adding additional lime juice or water. e) Transfer the dressing to a container or bottle. f) Keep in the fridge for up to three days. g) Before using it, give it a good shake.

113. Thai Peanut Dipping Sauce

Total Time: 5 minutes | Prep Time: 5 minutes

Ingredients:

	1/4 cup peanut butter
2 tablespoons soy sauce	1 tablespoon rice vinegar
1 tablespoon honey or maple syrup	1/2 teaspoon grated ginger
1 garlic clove, minced	1/4 cup water (adjust for consistency)

Directions:

a) In your Ninja Blast Max blender, mix together peanut butter, soy sauce, rice vinegar, honey, ginger, and garlic. b) Blend until smooth, 20–30 seconds on high. c) Add water little by little until the consistency of the sauce is what you want. d) If desired, add extra honey or soy sauce after tasting. e) You may use it as a dipping sauce for veggies, spring rolls, or meats that have been barbecued. f) For up to a week, keep it refrigerated in an airtight container.

114. Classic Caesar Dressing

Total Time: 10 minutes | Prep Time: 10 minutes

Ingredients:

	1/2 cup mayonnaise
2 tablespoons Dijon mustard	2 tablespoons lemon juice
2 tablespoons grated Parmesan cheese	1 garlic clove, minced
1 teaspoon anchovy paste (optional)	Salt and pepper, to taste

Directions:

a) Fill the Ninja Blast Max blender with mayonnaise, mustard, lemon juice, Parmesan, garlic, and anchovy paste (if using). b) Blend for 30 seconds at high speed or until smooth and fully integrated. c) If necessary, add extra lemon juice, salt, or pepper after tasting. d) The mixture should be transferred to a jar or other container, and then it should be placed in the refrigerator. e) Use as a roasted veggie dip or in salads. f) Store in the refrigerator for a maximum of one week.

115. Homemade Basil Pesto

Total Time: 10 minutes | Prep Time: 10 minutes

Ingredients:

	2 cups fresh basil leaves, packed
1/4 cup pine nuts (or walnuts)	1/2 cup grated Parmesan cheese
1 garlic clove	1/4 cup olive oil
Salt and pepper, to taste	

Directions:

a) In your Ninja Blast Max blender, add the garlic, Parmesan, pine nuts, and basil. b) For 15 to 20 seconds, blend on medium speed, scraping down the edges as necessary. c) Olive oil should be added gradually while the blender is running until the pesto achieves the consistency you want. d) Add salt and pepper to taste and adjust. e) For up to a week, keep it in the refrigerator after transferring it to a jar. f) Use as a sandwich spread or drizzle over roasted veggies or noodles.

116. Roasted Garlic Hummus

Total Time: 45 minutes | Prep Time: 10 minutes

Ingredients:

	1 head of garlic
1 can (15 oz) of chickpeas, drained and rinsed	1/4 cup tahini
1/4 cup lemon juice	1/4 cup olive oil
1/2 teaspoon ground cumin	Salt to taste
2 tablespoons water (adjust for consistency)	

Directions:

a) Set the oven's temperature to 400°F or 200°C. b) Slice off the top of the garlic bulb so that the cloves are visible, then cover with foil and olive oil. Bake for 35 to 40 minutes or until tender. c) Squeeze out the softened cloves of garlic after letting it cool somewhat. d) Add the chickpeas, tahini, lemon juice, cumin, salt, and roasted garlic to the Ninja Blast Max Blender. e) Add water as necessary to get the required consistency, and blend until smooth. f) Blend for a few more seconds after adding the olive oil. g) If necessary, taste and adjust the spices. h) Enjoy with pita or vegetables!

117. Carrot Ginger Soup

Total Time: 30 minutes | Prep Time: 10 minutes

Ingredients:

	4 medium carrots, peeled and chopped
1 tablespoon fresh ginger, minced	1 small onion, chopped
2 tablespoons olive oil	2 cups vegetable broth
1/2 cup coconut milk	Salt and pepper to taste

Directions:

a) In a large saucepan, bring the olive oil to a temperature of medium heat. After adding the onion, heat it for about five minutes or until it reaches the desired level of tenderness. b) Cook for a further five minutes, stirring periodically, after adding the carrots and ginger. c) Bring to a boil after adding the veggie broth. The carrots should be soft after 15 to 20 minutes of simmering over low heat. d) Blend the soup until it's smooth after transferring it to the Ninja Blast Max Blender. e) Stir the coconut milk into the broth after returning it to the stove. f) Add salt and pepper to taste and heat gently. g) Transfer to bowls and savour!

118. Zucchini Basil Soup

Total Time: 25 minutes | Prep Time: 10 minutes

Ingredients:

	3 medium zucchinis, chopped
1 small onion, chopped	2 tablespoons olive oil

2 cups vegetable broth	1/4 cup fresh basil leaves
Salt and pepper to taste	

Directions:

a) Heat the olive oil in a big saucepan over medium heat. Sauté the onion for five minutes until it becomes tender. b) Cook for a further five minutes after adding the chopped zucchini. c) Bring the mixture to a boil after adding the veggie broth. Simmer for ten minutes on low heat. d) Stir well after adding the fresh basil leaves. e) Blend the soup until it's smooth after transferring it to the Ninja Blast Max Blender. f) To taste, add salt and pepper. g) If preferred, top with more basil and serve warm.

119. Creamy Mushroom Soup

Total Time: 35 minutes | Prep Time: 10 minutes

Ingredients:

	1 pound mushrooms, sliced
1 small onion, chopped	2 tablespoons olive oil
2 cups vegetable broth	1/2 cup heavy cream
1 teaspoon thyme	Salt and pepper to taste

Directions:

a) Heat the olive oil in a big saucepan over medium heat. After adding the onion, cook it for five minutes. b) When the mushrooms have reached the desired tenderness and have shed their moisture, add the sliced mushrooms and continue to boil for around eight minutes. c) Bring to a simmer after adding the veggie broth. Give it ten minutes to cook. d) Season with salt, pepper, and thyme. e) Blend the soup until it's smooth after transferring it to the Ninja Blast Max Blender. f) To get a creamy texture, add the heavy cream and mix once more. g) If necessary, taste and adjust the spices. h) Garnish with fresh thyme and serve hot.

120. Choco-Banana Protein Pudding

Total Time: 10 minutes | Prep Time: 5 minutes

Ingredients:

	2 ripe bananas
2 tablespoons cocoa powder	1 scoop of chocolate protein powder
1/2 cup almond milk	1 teaspoon vanilla extract
A pinch of sea salt	

Directions:

a) After peeling, put the bananas in the Ninja Blast Max blender. b) A pinch of sea salt, almond milk, protein powder, cocoa powder, and vanilla essence should be added. c) On high, blend until creamy and smooth. d) If desired, add extra sweetness after tasting. e) After transferring to serving dishes, chill for two hours. f) Top with chocolate shavings, nuts, or sliced bananas if desired, and serve cold. g) Savour this nourishing and creamy delight!

121. Matcha Coconut Smoothie

Total Time: 5 minutes | Prep Time: 5 minutes

Ingredients:

	1 cup coconut milk (or almond milk)
1 tablespoon matcha powder	1 frozen banana
1/2 cup spinach (optional)	1 tablespoon honey or maple syrup (optional)
Ice cubes (optional for extra thickness)	

Directions:

a) In the Ninja Blast Max blender, combine the matcha powder and coconut milk. b) Add the spinach (if using) and frozen banana. c) If preferred, drizzle with maple syrup or honey for sweetness. d) If desired, thicken the smoothie by adding ice cubes. e) Over the course of roughly thirty seconds on high, blend until smooth and creamy. f) Transfer to a glass and serve right away. g) Savour the creamy coconut taste of this colourful green smoothie.

122. Chilled Melon Mint Soup

Total Time: 10 minutes | Prep Time: 10 minutes

Ingredients:

- 1 cup diced cantaloupe
- 3 cups diced watermelon
- Juice of 1 lime
- 1/4 cup fresh mint leaves
- Ice cubes
- 1 tablespoon honey (optional)

Directions:

a) In the blender, add the chopped cantaloupe, watermelon, and fresh mint leaves. b) If you want more sweetness, add the lime juice and honey. c) To cool the soup, add a few ice cubes. d) Blend until smooth and fully incorporated, about 1 minute on high. e) For more flavour, add additional mint or taste and adjust the sweetness. f) Before serving, pour the soup into bowls and let it cool for at least half an hour. g) Add a few more mint leaves as a garnish, and enjoy this cool summer salad.

123. Sun-Dried Tomato Hummus

Total Time: 10 minutes | Prep Time: 5 minutes

Ingredients:

- 1 can (15 oz) chickpeas, drained
- 1/2 cup sun-dried tomatoes
- 2 tablespoons olive oil
- Juice of 1 lemon
- 1/4 cup tahini
- 1 garlic clove
- Salt and pepper to taste
- Water (if needed to thin out the hummus)

Directions:

a) In the blender, combine the chickpeas, sun-dried tomatoes, tahini, garlic, and olive oil. b) The lemon juice should be squeezed in, and salt and pepper should be added to taste. c) If necessary, add a tablespoon of water at a time to get the desired consistency while blending on high until smooth. d) If desired, add additional salt, pepper, or lemon after tasting and adjusting the seasoning. e) Present the hummus in a bowl with crackers, pita chips, or fresh vegetables. f) Any leftovers may be kept in the fridge for up to three days in an airtight container.

124. Pineapple Spinach Power Smoothie

Total Time: 5 minutes | Prep Time: 5 minutes

Ingredients:

- 1/2 cup fresh spinach
- 1 cup fresh pineapple chunks
- 1 cup coconut water (or water)
- 1/2 banana (frozen for extra creaminess)
- Ice cubes (optional)
- 1 tablespoon chia seeds (optional)

Directions:

a) Put the frozen banana, spinach, and pineapple pieces in the blender. b) If using, add chia seeds and coconut water. c) To add cold and creaminess, add a couple of ice cubes. d) Blend till thick and smooth, 30 seconds on high. e) Enjoy the tropical, green power smoothie after pouring it into a glass. f) You may sprinkle some honey or maple syrup over top for added sweetness.

125. Blueberry Almond Butter Smoothie

Total Time: 5 minutes | Prep Time: 5 minutes

Ingredients:

- 1/2 cup frozen blueberries
- 1 tablespoon almond butter
- 1 cup almond milk (or milk of choice)
- 1/2 banana (optional for added creaminess)
- 1 teaspoon honey or maple syrup (optional)
- Ice cubes (optional)

Directions:

a) In the blender, combine the banana, almond milk, almond butter, and frozen blueberries. b) Additionally, honey or maple syrup may be added for sweetness if desired. c) For a cooler, thicker texture, add ice cubes. d) Blend until smooth, 30 seconds on high. e) Adjust sweetness according to taste. f) For a rich, antioxidant-rich smoothie, pour into a glass and serve right away.

126. Greek Yogurt Ranch Dressing

Total Time: 10 minutes | Prep Time: 10 minutes

Ingredients:

- 1 cup plain Greek yogurt
- 2 tbsp fresh lemon juice
- 1 tbsp dried parsley
- 1 tsp garlic powder
- 1 tsp onion powder
- 1 tsp dried dill
- Salt and pepper to taste

Directions:

a) The Greek yoghurt, lemon juice, parsley, onion powder, garlic powder, and dill should all be combined in a mixing dish. b) Mix well until all components are properly blended. c) To taste, add salt and pepper. d) One spoonful of water or milk at a time may be added to achieve the appropriate thickness for a thinner consistency. e) If needed, taste and adjust the spices. f) Serve right away or store in the fridge for up to a week.

127. Refreshing Watermelon Gazpacho

Total Time: 15 minutes | Prep Time: 15 minutes

Ingredients:

- 4 cups cubed watermelon
- 1 cucumber, peeled and chopped
- 1/2 red bell pepper, chopped
- 1/4 red onion, chopped
- 2 tbsp fresh lime juice
- 1 tbsp olive oil
- Salt and pepper to taste
- Fresh mint leaves for garnish (optional)

Directions:

a) Put the bell pepper, red onion, cucumber, and watermelon in your Ninja Blast Max blender. b) Blend on high for about thirty seconds or until the mixture is completely smooth. c) Blend once more to add the olive oil and lime juice. d) To taste, add salt and pepper. e) Add a little water to thin down the soup if it's too thick. f) Before serving, let it cool for 30 minutes. g) If desired, garnish with fresh mint leaves.

128. Creamy Broccoli Cheddar Soup

Total Time: 30 minutes | Prep Time: 10 minutes

Ingredients:

- 1/2 onion, chopped
- 2 cups broccoli florets
- 2 cups vegetable broth

1 cup shredded sharp cheddar cheese	1 cup milk or cream
1 tbsp olive oil	Salt and pepper to taste

Directions:

a) It is recommended that the chopped onion be sauteed in olive oil in a pot over medium heat until it becomes translucent throughout the cooking process. This should take around six minutes. b) Bring the vegetable stock and broccoli florets to a boil for 15 minutes or until the broccoli is soft. c) Fill your Ninja Blast Max Blender with the soup. d) On high, blend until creamy and smooth. e) Cheddar cheese that has been shredded should be added to the soup and stirred until it will melt. f) Add the cream or milk and mix everything together. g) Following the seasoning of the meal with salt and pepper to taste, it should be served warm.

129. Almond Butter Date Energy Shake

Total Time: 5 minutes | Prep Time: 5 minutes

Ingredients:

	1 cup unsweetened almond milk
2 tbsp almond butter	3 dates, pitted
1/2 tsp vanilla extract	1/4 tsp ground cinnamon
Ice cubes (optional)	

Directions:

a) Fill your Ninja Blast Max Blender with almond milk, almond butter, dates, vanilla essence, and ground cinnamon. b) Blend on high for approximately 30 seconds or until smooth and creamy. c) Add ice cubes and combine once more if you want your shake colder. d) If desired, add more dates to taste and adjust the sweetness. e) Transfer to a glass and serve right away.

130. Apple Pie Protein Smoothie

Total Time: 5 minutes | Prep Time: 5 minutes

Ingredients:

	1 medium apple, cored and chopped
1/2 banana	1/2 cup vanilla protein powder
1/2 tsp ground cinnamon	1/4 tsp ground nutmeg
1 cup unsweetened almond milk	Ice cubes (optional)

Directions:

a) In your Ninja Blast Max Blender, combine the apple, banana, almond milk, cinnamon, nutmeg, and vanilla protein powder. b) Blend for approximately 30 seconds on high or until smooth. c) Put in more ice cubes and give the smoothie another stir if you want it to be more thick and chilly. d) If required, add extra nutmeg or cinnamon after tasting and adjusting the seasonings. e) Transfer to a glass and savour!

131. Honeydew Cucumber Cooler

Total Time: 10 minutes | Prep Time: 10 minutes

Ingredients:

2 cups honeydew melon, chopped	1 cucumber, peeled and chopped
1 tablespoon fresh lime juice	1-2 teaspoons honey (optional)
1 cup cold water or coconut water	Ice cubes

Directions:

a) In the Ninja Blast Max Blender, combine the honeydew melon, cucumber, lime juice, honey, and water. b) Blend until it's smooth. c) If required, add extra honey after tasting to adjust sweetness. d) Pulse to smash the ice cubes until the appropriate consistency is achieved. e) If desired, top with lime wedges or cucumber slices after pouring into glasses. f) Serve right away and enjoy the cold, pleasant beverage!

132. Creamy Roasted Cauliflower Soup

Total Time: 30 minutes | Prep Time: 10 minutes

Ingredients:

	1 medium cauliflower, cut into florets
1 tablespoon olive oil	Salt and pepper to taste
1 small onion, chopped	2 garlic cloves, minced
2 cups vegetable broth	1/2 cup coconut milk
Fresh parsley for garnish	

Directions:

a) Four hundred degrees Fahrenheit, which is equivalent to 200 degrees Celsius, is the temperature that should be set for the oven. Before cooking the cauliflower florets, season them with salt, pepper, and olive oil. b) On a baking sheet, roast the cauliflower for 20 to 25 minutes or until it is soft and golden. c) Add the roasted cauliflower, coconut milk, vegetable broth, onion, and garlic to the Ninja Blast Max Blender. d) Blend till creamy and smooth. e) As necessary, add salt and pepper to taste and adjust the seasoning. f) After transferring the soup into dishes, sprinkle with fresh parsley. g) Enjoy it hot!

133. Vegan Chocolate Mousse

Total Time: 15 minutes | Prep Time: 15 minutes

Ingredients:

	1 ripe avocado, peeled and pitted
1/4 cup cocoa powder	1/4 cup maple syrup or agave syrup
1 teaspoon vanilla extract	Pinch of salt
2 tablespoons almond milk	Dark chocolate shavings (optional for garnish)

Directions:

a) In the Ninja Blast Max Blender, combine the avocado, almond milk, chocolate powder, maple syrup, vanilla extract, and salt. b) Blend till creamy and smooth. c) If desired, add more maple syrup after tasting to adjust sweetness. d) Scoop the mousse into serving plates when it has been mixed. e) To set, chill in the fridge for ten minutes. f) Before serving, sprinkle dark chocolate shavings over top. g) Enjoy cold!

134. Chilled Avocado Lime Soup

Total Time: 10 minutes | Prep Time: 10 minutes

Ingredients:

	2 ripe avocados, peeled and pitted
1 cup vegetable broth	1/4 cup fresh lime juice
1/2 teaspoon ground cumin	Salt and pepper to taste
Fresh cilantro for garnish	Ice cubes (optional)

Directions:

a) Fill the Ninja Blast Max Blender with avocados, ground cumin, lime juice, vegetable broth, salt, and pepper. b) Blend till creamy and smooth. c) To attain the right consistency, thin up the soup with a little additional veggie broth or ice cubes if it's too thick. d) Taste and add additional salt, pepper, or lime juice to suit the seasoning. e) After pouring the soup into bowls, let it sit in the fridge for ten minutes or so. f) Serve cool, garnished with fresh cilantro. g) Savour this cool, creamy soup!

135. Creamy Coconut Carrot Soup

Total Time: 30 minutes | Prep Time: 10 minutes

Ingredients:

	4 large carrots, peeled and chopped
1 tablespoon olive oil	1 small onion, chopped
2 garlic cloves, minced	1 teaspoon ground ginger
1 1/2 cups coconut milk	2 cups vegetable broth
Salt and pepper to taste	Fresh cilantro for garnish

Directions:

a) In a large saucepan, heat the olive oil over medium heat. Add the garlic and onion, and cook for approximately three minutes or until they are tender. b) Stir to coat after adding the diced carrots and ginger. c) Bring the vegetable broth to a boil after adding it. Carrots should be soft after 15 minutes of simmering over low heat. d) Before putting the soup in the Ninja Blast Max Blender, let it cool a little. e) Blend the coconut milk in the blender until it becomes creamy and smooth. f) Add salt and pepper to taste and adjust as necessary. g) After the soup has been poured into dishes, top with fresh cilantro. h) Enjoy the hearty soup while it's still warm!

136. Classic Tomato Basil Soup

Total Time: 30 minutes | Prep Time: 10 minutes

Ingredients:

	6 ripe tomatoes, chopped
1 small onion, chopped	2 cloves garlic, minced
2 cups vegetable broth	1 tablespoon olive oil
1 teaspoon dried basil	Salt and pepper, to taste
Fresh basil leaves for garnish	

Directions:

a) In a saucepan, heat the olive oil over medium heat. Cook the garlic and onion for three to four minutes or until they are tender. b) Cook for a further five minutes, stirring periodically, after adding the chopped tomatoes. c) Add the vegetable broth, salt, pepper, and dried basil. d) Bring to a boil, then reduce the heat to low and simmer for fifteen minutes. e) Puree the soup in the Ninja Blast Max Blender until it's smooth. f) Put the soup back in the saucepan and bring it to a boil. g) Use fresh basil leaves as a garnish, and serve the dish hot.

137. Lemon Tahini Dressing

Total Time: 10 minutes | Prep Time: 5 minutes

Ingredients:

	1/4 cup tahini
2 tablespoons fresh lemon juice	1 tablespoon olive oil
1 garlic clove, minced	2-3 tablespoons water (for desired consistency)
Salt and pepper, to taste	

Directions:

a) Put the tahini, lemon juice, olive oil, and garlic that has been minced into the Ninja Blast Max Blender and mix them together. On high, blend until creamy and smooth. b) To get the dressing consistency you want, add water a spoonful at a time. c) To taste, add salt and pepper. d) Use the dressing as a dip or drizzle it over salads. e) Keep leftovers in the refrigerator for up to five days in an airtight container.

138. Roasted Beet Hummus

Total Time: 40 minutes | Prep Time: 10 minutes

Ingredients:

	2 medium-sized roasted beets, peeled and chopped
1 can (15 oz) chickpeas, drained and rinsed	2 tablespoons tahini
1 tablespoon lemon juice	1 garlic clove
2 tablespoons olive oil	Salt and pepper, to taste

Directions:

a) Set the oven temperature to 400°F or 200°C. Beets should be soft after 30 minutes of roasting, wrapped in foil. b) Peel and cut the beets after letting them cool. c) In the Ninja Blast Max Blender, combine the roasted beets, chickpeas, tahini, garlic, lemon juice, and olive oil. d) To get the right texture, add water if necessary and blend until smooth. e) Add salt and pepper for seasoning. f) Serve with veggies or pita chips.

139. Turmeric Golden Milk Smoothie

Total Time: 10 minutes | Prep Time: 5 minutes

Ingredients:

	1 cup almond milk (or milk of choice)
1/2 teaspoon ground turmeric	1/4 teaspoon ground cinnamon
1 tablespoon honey (or maple syrup)	1/2 teaspoon vanilla extract
1/2 frozen banana	Pinch of black pepper (to activate turmeric)

Directions:

a) Fill the Ninja Blast Max Blender with almond milk, frozen banana, black pepper, turmeric, cinnamon, honey, and vanilla. b) On high, blend until creamy and smooth. c) If required, add extra honey after tasting to adjust sweetness. d) Transfer to a glass and serve cold. e) Top with more turmeric or cinnamon, if desired.

140. Chocolate Peanut Butter Shake

Total Time: 10 minutes | Prep Time: 5 minutes

Ingredients:

	1 banana (frozen)
1 cup milk (or milk alternative)	2 tablespoons peanut butter
1 tablespoon cocoa powder	1 tablespoon honey (or sweetener of choice)
1/4 teaspoon vanilla extract	Ice cubes (optional)

Directions:

a) Fill the Ninja Blast Max Blender with the frozen banana, milk, peanut butter, chocolate powder, honey, and vanilla extract. b) Blend till creamy and smooth. c) If you want a thicker texture, add ice cubes. d) Adjust sweetness according to taste. e) Pour into a glass and start drinking right away. f) If preferred, top with a drizzle of peanut butter or a few chocolate chips.

141. Cinnamon Apple Smoothie

Total Time: 5 minutes | Prep Time: 5 minutes

Ingredients:

	1 medium apple, cored and chopped
1/2 cup unsweetened almond milk	1/2 cup plain Greek yogurt
1 tablespoon honey	1/4 teaspoon ground cinnamon

1/2 teaspoon vanilla extract

Ice cubes (optional)

Directions:

a) Fill the Ninja Blast Max Blender with the apple, Greek yoghurt, almond milk, honey, cinnamon, and vanilla extract. b) If you want the smoothie to be colder, you may make it by adding a few ice cubes to it. c) Place the lid on the blender and process the mixture on high for thirty to sixty seconds or until it is completely smooth. d) If necessary, add extra honey to the smoothie after tasting it to regulate its sweetness. e) Transfer to a glass. f) Sprinkle some cinnamon on top as a garnish. g) Serve right away and savour!

142. Berry Beet Power Smoothie

Total Time: 5 minutes | Prep Time: 5 minutes

Ingredients:

1/2 cup frozen mixed berries	1 small beet, peeled and chopped
1/2 banana	1/2 cup coconut water
1 teaspoon fresh lemon juice	1 tablespoon chia seeds

Directions:

a) In the blender, combine the beet, banana, chia seeds, mixed berries, coconut water, and lemon juice. b) To get a creamy and smooth consistency, blend the ingredients on high for thirty to sixty seconds or until it achieves the desired consistency. c) Increase the amount of coconut water in the smoothie if it is too thick. d) Take a taste, and if necessary, adjust the amount of sweetness or lemon juice. e) Transfer to a glass and stir if necessary. f) Enjoy the power boost and serve cold!

143. Raspberry Chia Yogurt Bowl

Total Time: 10 minutes | Prep Time: 10 minutes

Ingredients:

1/2 cup frozen raspberries	1/2 cup plain Greek yogurt
1 tablespoon honey or maple syrup	1 tablespoon chia seeds
Fresh raspberries and granola for topping	1/4 teaspoon vanilla extract

Directions:

a) In the blender, combine the Greek yoghurt, chia seeds, frozen raspberries, honey, and vanilla essence. b) Blend until smooth, scraping down edges if needed, approximately 30 seconds on medium. c) Fill a basin with the combined ingredients. d) Add granola, honey or syrup, and fresh raspberries over top. e) To give the smoothie bowl more texture, mix in the toppings. f) Serve right now and enjoy your cool bowl!

144. Creamy Cashew Tomato Soup

Total Time: 15 minutes | Prep Time: 10 minutes

Ingredients:

2 cups diced tomatoes (fresh or canned)	1/2 cup raw cashews, soaked for at least 4 hours or overnight
1/2 cup vegetable broth	1/2 cup onion, chopped
1/2 teaspoon garlic powder	1/4 cup olive oil
Fresh basil for garnish	Salt and pepper to taste

Directions:

a) After draining, add the soaked cashews to the blender. b) Include the garlic powder, salt, pepper, tomatoes, onion, and vegetable broth in the mixture. Add the olive oil. c) For one to two minutes, blend on high or until the mixture is smooth and creamy. d) If needed, taste and adjust the seasoning. e) After pouring the soup into a saucepan, reheat it well over medium heat. f) Garnish with fresh basil and serve hot in bowls. g) Savour your luscious, creamy soup!

145. Cucumber Avocado Gazpacho

Total Time: 10 minutes | Prep Time: 10 minutes

Ingredients:

	1 cucumber, peeled and chopped
1 ripe avocado, peeled and pitted	1/2 cup red bell pepper, chopped
1/4 cup red onion, chopped	2 tablespoons fresh lime juice
1/2 teaspoon cumin	1/4 teaspoon salt
1 cup cold water	Fresh cilantro for garnish

Directions:

a) To make the smoothie, put the following ingredients into a blender: cucumber, avocado, red bell pepper, red onion, lime juice, cumin, salt, and cold water. Blend until very smooth. Blend until smooth. Blend until smooth. b) Blend until smooth and creamy, approximately 30 seconds on high. c) After tasting, make any required adjustments to the spices, such as adding additional cumin or lime juice for a more robust flavour. d) If you want your gazpacho cold, pour it into bowls and chill it for ten to fifteen minutes. e) Before serving, garnish with fresh cilantro. f) Serve this creamy, delicious gazpacho and savour it!

146. Sweet Potato Coconut Soup

Total Time: 30 minutes | Prep Time: 10 minutes

Ingredients:

	2 medium sweet potatoes, peeled and chopped
1 can (14 oz) coconut milk	1 cup vegetable broth
1/2 onion, chopped	2 cloves garlic, minced
1/2 tsp ground ginger	1/2 tsp ground cinnamon
Salt and pepper, to taste	

Directions:

a) Add the sweet potatoes, coconut milk, vegetable broth, ginger, garlic, onion, cinnamon, salt, and pepper to the Ninja Blast Max Blender. b) On high, blend until creamy and smooth. To get the right consistency, add a bit of additional broth if the mixture is too thick. c) Transfer the mixed mixture to a saucepan and cook, stirring regularly, over medium heat for 5 to 10 minutes. d) A taste should be taken, and if required, extra salt, pepper, or spices should be added to suit the flavouring. e) Serve in dishes once well hot, then dig in! f) If preferred, top with a coconut milk drizzle or a cinnamon sprinkle.

147. Spiced Mango Carrot Soup

Total Time: 25 minutes | Prep Time: 10 minutes

Ingredients:

	1 mango, peeled and chopped
2 medium carrots, peeled and chopped	1/2 onion, chopped
1 cup vegetable broth	1/2 cup coconut milk

1/2 tsp ground cumin	1/4 tsp ground coriander
Salt and pepper, to taste	

Directions:

a) In the Ninja Blast Max Blender, combine the mango, carrots, onion, coconut milk, vegetable broth, cumin, coriander, salt, and pepper. b) Blend until it's smooth. If the soup is too thick, you may add a little more vegetable broth. c) A pot should be used to hold the mixture, and it should be brought to a simmer over medium heat. d) To let the flavours mingle, simmer for 5 to 7 minutes, stirring periodically. e) As necessary, taste and adjust the seasoning. f) To serve the soup as soon as it is hot and ready, ladle it into bowls and serve it immediately.

DINNER RECIPES

148. Butternut Squash & Apple Soup

Total Time: 35 minutes | Prep Time: 10 minutes

Ingredients:

	1 small butternut squash, peeled and chopped
2 medium apples, peeled and chopped	1/2 onion, chopped
2 cups vegetable broth	1/2 cup coconut milk
1/4 tsp ground nutmeg	Salt and pepper, to taste

Directions:

a) Add the butternut squash, apples, onion, coconut milk, vegetable broth, nutmeg, salt, and pepper to your Ninja Blast Max Blender. b) Smoothly blend on high. c) Over medium heat, pour the mixed mixture into a saucepan and bring to a simmer. d) Cook until well cooked, stirring periodically, for 8 to 10 minutes. e) If needed, taste and add additional salt, pepper, or nutmeg to suit the seasoning. f) Serve the soup in bowls once it's hot and well combined, and feel free to add some fresh herbs as a garnish.

149. Broccoli Cheddar Soup

Total Time: 30 minutes | Prep Time: 10 minutes

Ingredients:

	2 cups broccoli florets
1/2 onion, chopped	1 1/2 cups vegetable broth
1 cup shredded cheddar cheese	1/2 cup milk
Salt and pepper, to taste	

Directions:

a) Fill the Ninja Blast Max Blender with vegetable broth, broccoli, and onion. b) If necessary, add milk gradually to get a creamy texture after blending until smooth. c) Pour the mixture into a saucepan and bring it to a simmer over medium heat. Continue to stir it occasionally. d) Add the shredded cheddar cheese and simmer until it melts and becomes smooth. e) Salt and pepper should be added to taste and adjusted accordingly. f) Serve the soup in dishes with more shredded cheese on top when it's cooked through and creamy.

150. Thai Coconut Curry Soup

Total Time: 30 minutes | Prep Time: 10 minutes

Ingredients:

	1 can (14 oz) coconut milk
1 cup vegetable broth	1 tbsp red curry paste
1/2 cup chopped carrots	1/2 cup chopped bell pepper
1/4 cup chopped cilantro	1 tbsp lime juice

Salt, to taste

Directions:

a) Add the carrots, bell pepper, cilantro, coconut milk, vegetable broth, red curry paste, lime juice, salt, and cilantro to your Ninja Blast Max blender. b) On high, blend until creamy and smooth. c) Over medium heat, pour the soup mixture into a saucepan and bring it to a boil. d) Allow the flavours to combine and the veggies to soften by cooking for 5 to 7 minutes. e) If necessary, add extra lime juice or salt to taste and adjust the seasoning. f) Serve the soup in bowls when it's cooked, and if you'd like, top with more cilantro and lime wedges.

151. Roasted Red Pepper Soup

Total Time: 30 minutes | Prep Time: 10 minutes

Ingredients:

	4 red bell peppers, halved and seeded
1 medium onion, chopped	2 cloves garlic, minced
2 tablespoons olive oil	4 cups vegetable broth
1 cup heavy cream	Salt and pepper to taste
Fresh basil for garnish (optional)	

Directions:

a) Set the oven temperature to 425°F (220°C). b) Arrange the red bell peppers, skin side up, on a baking sheet and roast until the skins are browned, about 20 minutes. c) Cook the garlic and onion in olive oil over medium heat for about five minutes or until they reach the desired level of tenderness while the peppers are roasting. d) After taking the peppers out of the oven, allow them to cool somewhat. Chop the peppers and remove the skins. e) Fill your Ninja Blender with the veggie broth, roasted peppers, sautéed onion and garlic, salt, and pepper. Blend until it's smooth. f) Pour the heavy cream into the soup after transferring it to a pot. Stirring periodically, cook over medium heat for 5 minutes. g) If preferred, top the hot soup with fresh basil.

152. Avocado Cilantro Soup

Total Time: 15 minutes | Prep Time: 10 minutes

Ingredients:

	2 ripe avocados, peeled and pitted
1 cup fresh cilantro leaves	1 small cucumber, peeled and chopped
1/2 cup Greek yogurt	2 cups vegetable broth
Juice of 1 lime	1/2 teaspoon cumin
Salt and pepper to taste	

Directions:

a) Add the avocados, cucumber, cilantro, Greek yoghurt, vegetable broth, lime juice, cumin, salt, and pepper to your Ninja Blender. b) Blend till creamy and smooth. c) If needed, taste and adjust the seasoning by adding extra lime juice or salt. d) For a cool soup, pour the soup into bowls and refrigerate for at least half an hour. e) Garnish with more cilantro leaves or a lime slice, and serve cold.

153. Sweet Potato & Peanut Soup

Total Time: 35 minutes | Prep Time: 10 minutes

Ingredients:

	2 medium sweet potatoes, peeled and chopped
1 small onion, chopped	2 cloves garlic, minced
1 tablespoon olive oil	4 cups vegetable broth

1/2 cup peanut butter	1/2 teaspoon ground ginger
Salt and pepper to taste	Chopped peanuts for garnish (optional)

Directions:

a) In a large saucepan, heat the olive oil over medium heat. Sauté the garlic and onion for three minutes or until they are tender. b) To the saucepan, add the vegetable broth and sliced sweet potatoes. Bring to a boil, then lower the heat and simmer until the sweet potatoes are soft, 15 to 20 minutes. c) Fill your Ninja Blender with the cooked sweet potatoes and broth. d) Add the ground ginger, peanut butter, salt, and pepper. Blend till creamy and smooth. e) Put the soup back in the pot and reheat it for five minutes over low heat. f) If preferred, top with chopped peanuts and serve hot.

154. Blender Chicken Alfredo

Total Time: 30 minutes | Prep Time: 10 minutes

Ingredients:

	2 boneless, skinless chicken breasts, cooked and chopped
2 cups heavy cream	1 cup grated Parmesan cheese
1/4 cup butter	2 cloves garlic, minced
1 teaspoon dried basil	Salt and pepper to taste
12 oz fettuccine pasta, cooked	

Directions:

a) Add the butter, garlic, dried basil, heavy cream, Parmesan cheese, salt, and pepper to your Ninja Blender. Blend until it's smooth. b) Transfer the mixture to a large pan and cook, stirring periodically, over medium heat for 5 to 7 minutes. c) Coat the cooked chicken with Alfredo sauce by adding it to the pan and stirring it around. d) To mix with the sauce, add the cooked fettuccine pasta to the pan and stir. e) Let the pasta absorb the sauce by simmering it for two to three minutes. f) If preferred, top the hot chicken Alfredo with more Parmesan cheese.

155. Creamy Pesto Pasta Sauce

Total Time: 15 minutes | Prep Time: 5 minutes

Ingredients:

	1 cup fresh basil leaves
1/2 cup Parmesan cheese	1/2 cup pine nuts
2 cloves garlic	1/4 cup olive oil
1/4 cup heavy cream	Salt and pepper to taste
12 oz pasta, cooked	

Directions:

a) Add the garlic, pine nuts, olive oil, salt, pepper, Parmesan cheese, and basil to your Ninja Blender. b) While blending, scrape down the sides of the bowl as necessary to ensure a smooth consistency. c) Blend the pesto one more until it becomes creamy after adding the heavy cream. d) After adding the creamy pesto sauce to a pan, cook it for two to three minutes over medium heat. e) Coat the cooked pasta with the pesto sauce by tossing it in the pan. f) If preferred, top the heated spaghetti with more Parmesan and fresh basil.

156. Zucchini & Walnut Pesto

Total Time: 10 minutes | Prep Time: 10 minutes

Ingredients:

	1 medium zucchini, chopped
1/2 cup walnuts, toasted	2 cloves garlic

1/2 cup fresh basil leaves	1/4 cup olive oil
1/4 cup nutritional yeast (or parmesan for non-vegan)	Salt and pepper to taste
Juice of 1/2 lemon	

Directions:

a) In your Ninja Blast Max blender, combine the zucchini, walnuts, garlic, basil, olive oil, nutritional yeast, salt, and pepper. b) On high, blend until the mixture is creamy and smooth. c) To make sure everything is completely mixed, scrape down the sides of the blender as necessary. d) If necessary, add additional salt, pepper, or lemon juice after tasting and adjusting the seasoning. e) Transfer to a bowl and serve right away or store in the refrigerator for later use. f) Savour it over roasted vegetables, spaghetti, or as a spread.

157. Spinach & Ricotta Stuffed Shells

Total Time: 35 minutes | Prep Time: 15 minutes

Ingredients:

	20 jumbo pasta shells
1 1/2 cups ricotta cheese	2 cups fresh spinach, wilted and chopped
1/2 cup shredded mozzarella	1/4 cup grated parmesan
1 egg	1/4 teaspoon nutmeg
Salt and pepper to taste	1 jar marinara sauce

Directions:

a) If you want to cook the big pasta shells, be sure to follow the instructions on the package. After draining, put it away. b) Add the ricotta, spinach, mozzarella, parmesan, egg, nutmeg, salt, and pepper to your blender. c) Blend until completely combined and smooth. d) Set the oven temperature to 375°F, or 190°C. e) Place the spinach-ricotta mixture into the prepared pasta shells. f) Line the bottom of a baking dish with marinara sauce. g) Place the filled shells on the plate and pour more marinara sauce over them. h) Bake for 20 minutes, until the top is brown and bubbling.

158. Vegan Cashew Cheese Sauce

Total Time: 10 minutes | Prep Time: 10 minutes

Ingredients:

	1 cup raw cashews, soaked for 4 hours or overnight
1/2 cup water	2 tablespoons nutritional yeast
1 tablespoon lemon juice	1 garlic clove
1/2 teaspoon turmeric	Salt to taste

Directions:

a) After draining, add the soaked cashews to your blender. b) Add salt, turmeric, lemon juice, water, nutritional yeast, and garlic. c) On high, blend until the sauce is creamy and fully smooth. d) If desired, add extra lemon juice or salt to taste and adjust the seasoning. e) Serve as a chip dip or as a topping for spaghetti or roasted vegetables. f) Keep leftovers in the refrigerator for up to five days in an airtight container.

159. Spicy Roasted Tomato Salsa

Total Time: 20 minutes | Prep Time: 10 minutes

Ingredients:

	4 medium tomatoes, halved
1 small onion, quartered	2 cloves garlic
1 jalapeño, seeds removed for less heat	1 tablespoon olive oil

1/2 teaspoon cumin

1/2 teaspoon chilli powder

Salt and pepper to taste

Juice of 1 lime

Fresh cilantro for garnish

Directions:

a) Set the oven temperature to 400°F or 200°C. b) Drizzle olive oil over the tomatoes, onion, garlic, and jalapeño on a baking sheet. c) Roast until the tomatoes are tender and browned, 15 to 20 minutes. d) Take it out of the oven and give it some time to cool. e) In your blender, combine the roasted veggies, lime juice, cumin, chilli powder, and salt & pepper. f) To get the desired salsa consistency—chunky or smooth—blend on low. g) Serve with tacos or tortilla chips and garnish with fresh cilantro.

160. Blender Enchilada Sauce

Total Time: 15 minutes | Prep Time: 10 minutes

Ingredients:

2 tablespoons olive oil

1 small onion, chopped

2 cloves garlic, minced

1 can (14 oz) tomato sauce

1/2 cup vegetable broth

1 tablespoon chilli powder

1 teaspoon cumin

1/2 teaspoon paprika

1/4 teaspoon cayenne pepper (optional)

Salt to taste

Directions:

a) In a small pan, heat the olive oil over medium heat. b) Cook for about five minutes after adding the chopped onion and garlic until they are tender. c) Add the tomato sauce, vegetable broth, cumin, paprika, cayenne, chilli powder, and salt to your blender. d) Put the garlic and sautéed onion in the blender and process until smooth. e) If necessary, add extra salt or chilli powder to taste and adjust the seasoning. f) To thicken the sauce, put it in a pot and cook it for five minutes. g) Serve as a dipping sauce or on tacos or enchiladas.

161. Creamy Garlic Parmesan Sauce

Total Time: 10 minutes | Prep Time: 10 minutes

Ingredients:

1/2 cup heavy cream

1/2 cup grated Parmesan cheese

2 tbsp butter

3 cloves garlic, minced

1/4 tsp salt

1/4 tsp black pepper

1 tbsp chopped parsley (optional)

Directions:

a) Add butter, garlic, Parmesan cheese, heavy cream, salt, and pepper to your Ninja Blast Max Blender. b) Blend for 30 seconds on high or until the mixture is creamy and smooth. c) Heat the sauce over medium heat after pouring it into a small saucepan. d) Simmer for two to three minutes, stirring periodically, until slightly thickened. e) As necessary, taste and adjust the seasoning. f) Serve warm over chicken, pasta, or veggies and garnish with chopped parsley if preferred.

162. Chipotle Lime Dressing

Total Time: 5 minutes | Prep Time: 5 minutes

Ingredients:

1/2 cup olive oil

1/4 cup lime juice

1 chipotle pepper in adobo sauce

1 tbsp adobo sauce

1 tbsp honey

1/4 tsp garlic powder

Salt and pepper to taste

Directions:

a) Add the following ingredients to your Ninja Blast Max Blender: olive oil, lime juice, chipotle pepper, adobo sauce, honey, garlic powder, salt, and pepper. b) Blend until smooth, 20–30 seconds on high. c) If necessary, adjust the seasoning by tasting and adding extra honey or salt for balance. d) Take the dressing and place it in a jar or other container. e) For up to a week, keep in the refrigerator. f) Pour over roasted veggies, grilled poultry, or salads.

163. Mango Habanero Salsa

Total Time: 10 minutes | Prep Time: 10 minutes

Ingredients:

	1 ripe mango, peeled and chopped
1 small red onion, chopped	1 habanero pepper, seeds removed
1/4 cup cilantro, chopped	2 tbsp lime juice
1/4 tsp salt	1/4 tsp black pepper

Directions:

a) Put the following ingredients in your Ninja Blast Max Blender: mango, onion, habanero pepper, cilantro, lime juice, salt, and pepper. b) Pulse until you have the chunky or smooth salsa consistency you like. c) If needed, taste and adjust the seasoning. d) Before serving, move to a bowl and chill for ten minutes. e) Serve with tacos, grilled meats, or tortilla chips.

164. Blender Meatball Marinara

Total Time: 20 minutes | Prep Time: 15 minutes

Ingredients:

	1 lb ground beef or turkey
1/2 cup breadcrumbs	1/4 cup grated Parmesan cheese
1 egg	2 tbsp fresh parsley, chopped
1/2 tsp garlic powder	1/4 tsp salt
1/4 tsp black pepper	1 jar marinara sauce (24 oz)

Directions:

a) Ground beef, breadcrumbs, egg, parsley, garlic powder, Parmesan cheese, salt, and pepper should all be combined in a big dish. Stir until everything is well blended. b) Form the mixture into tiny, one-inch-diameter meatballs. c) The meatballs should be browned on all sides after 7 to 8 minutes of cooking in a large pan over medium heat, flipping periodically. d) To smooth up the marinara sauce, pour it into your Ninja Blast Max Blender and mix for 20 to 30 seconds. e) Simmer the meatballs in the pan for an additional five minutes after adding the blended marinara sauce. f) Serve hot on a sub bun for a meatball sandwich or with pasta.

165. Spaghetti with Blender Vodka Sauce

Total Time: 25 minutes | Prep Time: 10 minutes

Ingredients:

	1 lb spaghetti
2 tbsp olive oil	1/2 onion, chopped
3 cloves garlic, minced	1 can (14.5 oz) crushed tomatoes
1/4 cup vodka	1/2 cup heavy cream
1/4 tsp red pepper flakes (optional)	Salt and pepper to taste
Fresh basil for garnish	

Directions:

a) In order to cook the pasta, be sure to follow the instructions on the box. After it has been drained, dispose of it. b) After the olive oil has been heated, add the chopped onion and garlic to the pan, and then adjust the heat to medium. Stir the mixture carefully. Sauté for 3-4 minutes, or until the garlic and onion are tender. c) Fill your Ninja Blast Max Blender with smashed tomatoes, vodka, heavy cream, salt, pepper, and red pepper flakes (if using). d) Blend until smooth, 30 seconds on high. e) After adding the blended sauce to the pan, simmer it for five to seven minutes over low heat, stirring now and again. f) Coat the cooked spaghetti evenly by tossing it in the sauce. g) Serve hot, garnished with fresh basil.

166. Blender Bolognese Sauce

Total Time: 45 minutes | Prep Time: 10 minutes

Ingredients:

	1 lb ground beef
1 medium onion, chopped	2 cloves garlic, minced
1 (28 oz) can crushed tomatoes	1 (6 oz) can tomato paste
1 cup beef broth	1 tsp dried oregano
1 tsp dried basil	Salt and pepper, to taste
2 tbsp olive oil	1/4 cup heavy cream (optional)

Directions:

a) In a large pan, heat the olive oil over medium heat. Add the garlic, onion, and ground meat. Maintain the cooking process for the meat, breaking it up as it cooks until the skin of the meat has become brown. b) Add the crushed tomatoes, tomato paste, beef broth, oregano, basil, salt, and pepper to the Ninja Blast Max Blender. c) Run the blender on low speed until the sauce is fully mixed and smooth. d) Stir the meat mixture in the pan after adding the blended sauce. e) The sauce should be brought to a boil and then cooked for twenty minutes while being stirred at regular intervals. f) Add heavy cream if you like a creamier sauce. Mix thoroughly. g) You may use it for lasagna or serve it over your preferred pasta.

167. Creamy Cajun Shrimp Pasta

Total Time: 30 minutes | Prep Time: 10 minutes

Ingredients:

	1 lb shrimp, peeled and deveined
2 tbsp Cajun seasoning	8 oz fettuccine pasta
1/2 cup heavy cream	1/2 cup chicken broth
2 tbsp butter	1 small onion, chopped
2 cloves garlic, minced	1/2 cup grated Parmesan cheese
Salt and pepper, to taste	

Directions:

a) Follow the directions on the box to prepare the fettuccine pasta. After draining, put it away. b) Add salt, pepper, and Cajun spice to the shrimp. c) Melt the butter in a big pan over a medium heat. Add the shrimp and simmer for 3-4 minutes or until pink. After taking the shrimp out of the pan, put them aside. d) Additionally, add the onion and garlic to the same skillet. Sauté for approximately 3 minutes or until softened. e) Add the chicken broth, Parmesan, and heavy cream to the Ninja Blast Max Blender. To combine, blend on low. f) Fill the pan with the blended cream mixture and heat it until it simmers. Cook for five minutes. g) Toss to cover everything in the sauce after adding the cooked pasta and shrimp to the pan. h) Garnish with Cajun flavour and more Parmesan cheese.

168. Chimichurri Marinated Steak

Total Time: 2 hours | Prep Time: 15 minutes

Ingredients:

- 2 ribeye steaks (or your preferred cut)
- 1/4 cup fresh parsley, chopped
- 1/4 cup fresh cilantro, chopped
- 2 cloves garlic, minced
- 2 tbsp red wine vinegar
- 1/4 cup olive oil
- 1/2 tsp red pepper flakes
- Salt and pepper, to taste

Directions:

a) To the Ninja Blast Max Blender, add the chopped parsley, cilantro, garlic, red wine vinegar, olive oil, crushed red pepper flakes, and seasonings of your choice. Blend until smooth. Blend until it's smooth. b) Put the steaks in a shallow dish or a plastic bag that can be sealed. Make sure the steaks are well covered with the chimichurri marinade. Marinate overnight or for at least an hour. c) Heat your skillet or grill to a medium-high temperature. d) After taking the steaks out of the marinade, add more salt and pepper to taste. e) To achieve medium-rare, grill or broil the steaks for 4–6 minutes on each side. f) Before slicing, let the steaks rest for five minutes. g) Drizzle more chimichurri sauce over the dish.

169. Teriyaki Chicken Stir-Fry

Total Time: 25 minutes | Prep Time: 10 minutes

Ingredients:

- 2 chicken breasts, sliced thin
- 1 bell pepper, sliced
- 1 carrot, julienned
- 1/2 cup broccoli florets
- 1/4 cup soy sauce
- 2 tbsp honey
- 1 tbsp rice vinegar
- 1 tbsp cornstarch
- 1/4 cup water
- 1 tbsp sesame oil
- 2 cloves garlic, minced

Directions:

a) Add soy sauce, honey, rice vinegar, cornstarch, and water to the Ninja Blast Max Blender. Blend till smooth on low. b) In a big skillet or wok, heat the sesame oil over medium heat. Sauté the garlic for one minute. c) Cook the chicken in the pan for approximately 6–7 minutes or until browned. d) Stir-fry the broccoli, carrot, and bell pepper for a further five minutes or until the veggies are soft. e) Stir well after adding the teriyaki sauce to the pan from the blender. f) Give the sauce two to three minutes to thicken, stirring now and again. g) For a full supper, serve the stir-fry over noodles or rice.

170. Thai Peanut Noodle Bowl

Total Time: 20 minutes | Prep Time: 10 minutes

Ingredients:

- 8 oz rice noodles
- 1/2 cup peanut butter
- 2 tbsp soy sauce
- 1 tbsp lime juice
- 1 tbsp sesame oil
- 1 tsp honey
- 1/2 tsp ginger, grated
- 1/4 cup water
- 1/4 cup chopped green onions
- 1/4 cup crushed peanuts (optional)
- 1/2 cup shredded carrots

Directions:

a) When it comes to cooking the rice noodles, be sure to follow the instructions on the package. After draining, put it away. b) Add peanut butter, soy sauce, lime juice, sesame oil, honey, ginger, and water to the Ninja Blast Max Blender. On low, blend until creamy and smooth. c) Coat the cooked noodles well by tossing them with the peanut sauce. d) Add the green onions, crushed peanuts (if using), and shredded carrots. e) For the last mix, combine everything. f) Garnish with crushed peanuts for crunch or more green onions, and serve in bowls.

171. Cashew Cream Vegan Alfredo

Total Time: 15 minutes | Prep Time: 10 minutes

Ingredients:

	1 cup raw cashews, soaked
1 cup water	2 tbsp nutritional yeast
2 tbsp olive oil	1 garlic clove
1 tbsp lemon juice	1/2 tsp salt
Freshly ground pepper, to taste	12 oz fettuccine pasta, cooked

Directions:

a) Put the cashews that have been soaked in water, nutritional yeast, olive oil, lemon juice, garlic, salt, and pepper into your Ninja Blast Max blender. b) On high, blend until creamy and smooth. c) If necessary, add extra salt or pepper after tasting and adjusting the seasoning. d) Coat the cooked pasta completely by tossing it with the cashew cream sauce. e) Garnish with fresh vegetables or herbs and serve right away. f) Optional: For extra taste, add sautéed spinach or mushrooms.

172. Curried Lentil & Chickpea Bowl

Total Time: 25 minutes | Prep Time: 10 minutes

Ingredients:

	1 cup dried lentils, rinsed
1 can (15 oz) chickpeas, drained and rinsed	1 can (15 oz) coconut milk
1 tbsp curry powder	1 tsp turmeric
1 tbsp olive oil	1 onion, chopped
1 garlic clove, minced	2 cups vegetable broth
Salt and pepper to taste	

Directions:

a) In a large saucepan, heat the olive oil over medium heat. Add the garlic and onion and sauté until they are tender. b) Stir in the turmeric and curry powder until aromatic. c) To the saucepan, add the chickpeas, lentils, coconut milk, and vegetable broth. d) Bring to a boil, then lower the heat to a simmer and cook until the lentils are soft about 20 minutes. e) To taste, add salt and pepper. f) To finish, sprinkle the lentil and chickpea mixture with lime juice and fresh cilantro and arrange it in individual bowls.

173. Creamy Sun-Dried Tomato Pasta

Total Time: 20 minutes | Prep Time: 10 minutes

Ingredients:

	8 oz pasta of choice
1/2 cup sun-dried tomatoes packed in oil	1/2 cup cashews, soaked
1/2 cup water	1 tbsp nutritional yeast
1 garlic clove	2 tbsp olive oil
Salt and pepper, to taste	

Directions:

a) Follow the directions on the pasta box to cook it. b) Add the sun-dried tomatoes, soaked cashews, water, nutritional yeast, garlic, and olive oil to your blender while the pasta cooks. c) On high, blend until creamy and smooth. d) After draining, put the pasta back in the saucepan. e) Cover the spaghetti with the smooth, sun-dried tomato sauce and toss to cover. f) After seasoning the meat with salt and pepper, it should be served with fresh basil and either standard or vegan Parmesan cheese. Fresh basil is particularly delicious.

174. Roasted Cauliflower & Garlic Soup

Total Time: 40 minutes | Prep Time: 10 minutes

Ingredients:

	1 medium cauliflower, cut into florets
1 onion, chopped	4 garlic cloves, peeled
1 tbsp olive oil	4 cups vegetable broth
1/2 cup coconut milk	Salt and pepper, to taste

Directions:

a) Set the oven temperature to 400°F or 200°C. Roast the cauliflower florets, onion, and garlic cloves for 25 to 30 minutes or until they are soft and golden. Toss them with olive oil. b) Put the coconut milk, vegetable broth, and roasted cauliflower combination in a blender. c) Smoothly blend on high. d) Return the soup to a saucepan and cook it over medium heat. e) To taste, add salt and pepper. f) Garnish with fresh herbs or drizzle with olive oil and serve hot.

175. Blender Pizza Sauce

Total Time: 10 minutes | Prep Time: 5 minutes

Ingredients:

	1 can (15 oz) crushed tomatoes
1 tbsp olive oil	1 tsp dried oregano
1 tsp garlic powder	1/2 tsp red pepper flakes (optional)
Salt and pepper, to taste	

Directions:

a) Put the mashed tomatoes, olive oil, oregano, garlic powder, red pepper flakes, salt, and pepper into your Ninja Blast Max blender. Blend until smooth. b) Blend at a medium speed until everything is completely combined and smooth. c) If needed, taste and adjust the seasoning. d) Move to a saucepan and reheat through over low heat. e) Store in the fridge for up to a week or use right away on pizza.

176. Vegan Mac & Cheese Sauce

Total Time: 15 minutes | Prep Time: 10 minutes

Ingredients:

	1 cup cashews (soaked for 2 hours)
1/2 cup nutritional yeast	1/4 cup lemon juice
1/2 cup water	1 tsp garlic powder
1 tsp onion powder	1/2 tsp turmeric
Salt and pepper to taste	

Directions:

a) After soaking, drain and rinse the cashews. b) In the Ninja Blast Max blender, combine the cashews, nutritional yeast, lemon juice, water, turmeric, and onion and garlic powders. c) On high, blend until creamy and smooth. d) Salt and pepper should be added to taste, but only if required. e) You may adjust the sauce's consistency by adding a bit more water if it's too thick. f) Use as a vegetable dip or drizzle over cooked spaghetti.

177. Spicy Blender Tofu Marinade

Total Time: 10 minutes | Prep Time: 5 minutes

Ingredients:

	1/4 cup soy sauce
2 tbsp rice vinegar	2 tbsp sriracha sauce
1 tbsp maple syrup	1 tbsp sesame oil
2 cloves garlic, minced	1 tsp fresh ginger, grated

1 block firm tofu (pressed and cubed)

Directions:

a) Soy sauce, rice vinegar, sriracha, maple syrup, sesame oil, ginger, and garlic should all be combined in the Ninja Blast Max blender. b) Blend until well mixed and smooth. c) Put the diced tofu in a zip-top bag or a shallow dish. d) After adding the marinade, gently toss the tofu to coat it. e) For added flavour, marinate for at least 30 minutes or overnight. f) Once marinated, cook the tofu in a stir-fry grill or oven.

178. Cilantro Lime Chicken Marinade

Total Time: 15 minutes | Prep Time: 10 minutes

Ingredients:

1/4 cup lime juice (freshly squeezed)	1/2 cup fresh cilantro, chopped
2 cloves garlic, minced	2 tbsp olive oil
1/2 tsp chilli powder	1 tsp ground cumin
2 chicken breasts (boneless, skinless)	Salt and pepper to taste

Directions:

a) In the Ninja Blast Max blender, combine the cilantro, lime juice, olive oil, cumin, garlic, chilli powder, salt, and pepper. b) Blend until blended and smooth. c) Cover the chicken breasts in a shallow dish or zip-top bag with the marinade. d) For optimal taste, seal and chill for at least 30 minutes or up to 4 hours. e) Heat your skillet or grill to a medium temperature. f) The chicken should be cooked through after grilling for 6–7 minutes on each side.

179. Chipotle Ranch Dressing

Total Time: 10 minutes | Prep Time: 5 minutes

Ingredients:

1/2 cup sour cream	1/2 cup mayonnaise
1 chipotle pepper in adobo sauce	1/4 cup buttermilk
1 tsp onion powder	1 tsp garlic powder
	Salt and pepper to taste

Directions:

a) Fill the Ninja Blast Max blender with mayonnaise, sour cream, buttermilk, chipotle pepper, adobo sauce, garlic powder, and onion powder. b) On high, blend until creamy and smooth. c) Salt and pepper should be used to taste and adjust the seasoning as necessary. Add extra adobo sauce or another chipotle pepper if you want it hotter. d) To allow the flavours to merge, pour into a jar or bottle and place in the refrigerator for at least half an hour. e) Use as a dip for vegetables and chips or as a dressing for salads.

180. Italian Herb Blender Dressing

Total Time: 10 minutes | Prep Time: 5 minutes

Ingredients:

1/4 cup red wine vinegar	1/2 cup olive oil
1 tsp dried oregano	2 tbsp Dijon mustard
1/2 tsp garlic powder	1 tsp dried basil
	Salt and pepper to taste

Directions:

a) Put the following ingredients into the Ninja Blast Max blender: olive oil, red wine vinegar, Dijon mustard, oregano, basil, garlic powder, salt, and pepper. Blend these items until smooth. b) Blend until emulsified and smooth. c) If necessary, taste and adjust the seasoning. d) To store, pour into a bottle or jar. e) Keep in the fridge for up to a week. f) Use as a marinade for meats and vegetables or drizzle over salads.

181. Blender Gazpacho

Total Time: 15 minutes | Prep Time: 10 minutes

Ingredients:

	4 ripe tomatoes, chopped
1 cucumber, peeled and chopped	1 bell pepper, chopped
1 small red onion, chopped	2 cups tomato juice
2 tbsp red wine vinegar	2 tbsp olive oil
1 tsp garlic, minced	Salt and pepper to taste
Fresh basil leaves for garnish	

Directions:

a) To the Ninja Blast Max Blender, add the bell pepper, tomatoes, cucumber, red onion, and garlic. b) Add the olive oil, tomato juice, and red wine vinegar. c) Add salt and pepper for seasoning. d) Smoothly blend on high. e) If needed, taste and adjust the seasoning. f) Garnish with fresh basil leaves and serve in dishes. g) If you want your soup cold, chill it in the fridge for half an hour.

182. Korean BBQ Beef Marinade

Total Time: 1 hour 10 minutes | Prep Time: 10 minutes

Ingredients:

	1/4 cup soy sauce
2 tbsp sesame oil	2 tbsp brown sugar
2 cloves garlic, minced	1 tbsp grated ginger
2 tbsp rice vinegar	1 tbsp gochujang (Korean chilli paste)
1 tbsp sesame seeds	1/4 cup green onions, chopped

Directions:

a) Soy sauce, sesame oil, brown sugar, rice vinegar, ginger, garlic, gochujang, sesame seeds, and green onions should all be combined in a blender. b) To combine everything, blend on low. c) In a shallow dish, cover meat (such as short ribs or flank steak) with the marinade. d) For at least an hour, cover and chill (or overnight for additional flavour). e) To achieve the proper doneness, sear or grill the marinated meat over medium-high heat. f) Serve with veggies or rice after slicing thinly.

183. Garlic Butter Shrimp Pasta

Total Time: 20 minutes | Prep Time: 10 minutes

Ingredients:

	1 lb shrimp, peeled and deveined
8 oz spaghetti or your choice of pasta	4 tbsp unsalted butter
4 garlic cloves, minced	1/2 cup chicken broth
1/4 cup Parmesan cheese, grated	1 tbsp fresh parsley, chopped
Salt and pepper to taste	

Directions:

a) Pasta should be cooked as directed on the box, drained, and left aside. b) Melt the butter in a big pan over a medium heat. c) Sauté the garlic for one minute till it becomes aromatic. d) Cook the shrimp in the pan for three to four minutes or until they are opaque and pink. e) After adding the chicken broth, boil it for two minutes. f) Add the cooked pasta, parsley, and Parmesan cheese. g) Prepare the dish immediately after seasoning it to taste with salt and pepper.

184. Greek Yogurt Tzatziki Sauce

Total Time: 10 minutes | Prep Time: 10 minutes

Ingredients:

	1 cup Greek yogurt
1 cucumber, grated and excess water squeezed out	2 tbsp olive oil
1 tbsp lemon juice	1 tbsp fresh dill, chopped
2 cloves garlic, minced	Salt and pepper to taste

Directions:

a) Fill the Ninja Blast Max Blender with Greek yoghurt, grated cucumber, lemon juice, olive oil, garlic, and dill. b) On low, blend until smooth and thoroughly mixed. c) Season with salt and pepper after tasting. d) Before serving, let it cool for half an hour in the fridge. e) Serve as a vegetable dip, with pita bread, or with grilled meats.

185. Avocado Ranch Dressing

Total Time: 5 minutes | Prep Time: 5 minutes

Ingredients:

	1 ripe avocado, peeled and pitted
1/2 cup buttermilk	1/4 cup mayonnaise
1 tbsp fresh lemon juice	1 tsp garlic powder
1 tsp onion powder	1 tbsp fresh parsley, chopped
Salt and pepper to taste	

Directions:

a) In the blender, combine the avocado, buttermilk, mayonnaise, lemon juice, onion powder, and garlic powder. b) On high, blend until creamy and smooth. c) Pulse to mix in the parsley, salt, and pepper. d) As necessary, taste and adjust the seasoning. e) To let the flavours blend, pour into a container or jar and place in the refrigerator for half an hour. f) The dip may be used for veggies or chips, or it can be placed on top of salads.

186. Lemon Herb Salmon Marinade

Total Time: 15 minutes | Prep Time: 15 minutes

Ingredients:

	4 salmon fillets
1/4 cup olive oil	2 tablespoons lemon juice
2 cloves garlic, minced	1 teaspoon dried thyme
1 teaspoon dried rosemary	Salt and pepper to taste
1 teaspoon lemon zest	

Directions:

a) Whisk together the lemon zest, olive oil, lemon juice, minced garlic, thyme, rosemary, salt, and pepper in a small bowl. b) Put the salmon fillets in a plastic bag that can be sealed or on a shallow plate. c) Make sure the salmon is well covered by pouring the marinade over it. d) For optimal taste, cover and chill for 30 to 60 minutes. e) Heat a nonstick skillet or grill to a medium temperature. f) If you grill or cook the salmon for four to five minutes on each side, it should be easy to flake apart with a fork.

187. Creamy Roasted Corn Soup

Total Time: 40 minutes | Prep Time: 10 minutes

Ingredients:

	4 cups fresh or frozen corn kernels

1 tablespoon olive oil	1 onion, chopped
2 cloves garlic, minced	1 medium potato, peeled and diced
4 cups vegetable broth	1 cup coconut milk
Salt and pepper to taste	Fresh parsley for garnish

Directions:

a) Set the oven's temperature to 400°F or 200°C. b) Line a baking sheet with corn and roast for 20 to 25 minutes, stirring occasionally. c) The olive oil should be placed in a big saucepan and heated over medium heat until it reaches the desired temperature. Cook the chopped onion and garlic for around five minutes or until they are tender. d) Following the addition of the vegetable stock, the diced potato, and the roasted corn, bring the saucepan to a boiling temperature. e) Once the heat has been reduced to a simmer, continue cooking the potato for ten to fifteen minutes longer or until it reaches the desired level of doneness. f) Blend the soup in your Ninja Blast Max Blender until it's creamy and smooth. g) Add salt, pepper, and coconut milk and stir. Five more minutes should be spent heating the soup. h) Garnish with fresh parsley and serve hot.

188. Spiced Pumpkin Soup

Total Time: 45 minutes | Prep Time: 15 minutes

Ingredients:

	2 cups pumpkin puree
1 tablespoon olive oil	1 onion, chopped
2 cloves garlic, minced	1 teaspoon ground cumin
1/2 teaspoon ground cinnamon	1/2 teaspoon ground ginger
1/2 teaspoon chilli powder	4 cups vegetable broth
1/2 cup coconut cream	Salt and pepper to taste

Directions:

a) Heat the olive oil in a large saucepan over medium heat. Sauté the chopped garlic and onion for about five minutes or until they are tender. b) Add the chilli powder, ginger, cinnamon, and cumin and simmer for 1 minute until aromatic. c) Stir together the vegetable broth and pumpkin puree after adding them to the saucepan. d) The soup should be cooked for twenty minutes after it has been brought to a boil, after which the heat should be reduced to a simmer. e) Blend the soup with your Ninja Blast Max Blender until it's smooth. f) After adding the coconut cream, salt, and pepper, simmer for five more minutes. g) If preferred, top the heated dish with a swirl of more coconut cream.

189. Buffalo Cauliflower Bites

Total Time: 30 minutes | Prep Time: 10 minutes

Ingredients:

	1 medium cauliflower, cut into florets
1/2 cup all-purpose flour	1/2 cup water
1/2 teaspoon garlic powder	1/2 teaspoon paprika
Salt and pepper to taste	1/2 cup buffalo sauce
2 tablespoons olive oil	Fresh parsley for garnish

Directions:

a) Put parchment paper on a baking pan and preheat the oven to 400°F (200°C). b) When you are ready to make the batter, take a bowl and combine the flour, water, paprika, garlic powder, salt, and pepper. Mix all of these ingredients together completely. c) The cauliflower florets should be placed on the baking sheet after the batter has been applied around each one of them fully. d) Bake the cauliflower for twenty to twenty-five minutes, flipping it over halfway through the cooking process. e) While the cauliflower is roasting, bring the buffalo sauce and olive oil to a simmer in a small skillet over medium heat. This should be done while the cauliflower is baking. f) Take the cauliflower out of the oven when it's crispy and mix it with the buffalo sauce. g) Put the coated cauliflower back in the oven for five more minutes. h) Garnish with fresh parsley and serve hot.

190. Mexican Street Corn Soup

Total Time: 35 minutes | Prep Time: 10 minutes

Ingredients:

	4 cups corn kernels (fresh or frozen)
2 tablespoons butter	1/2 cup diced onion
2 cloves garlic, minced	1/2 teaspoon smoked paprika
1/4 teaspoon chilli powder	4 cups chicken or vegetable broth
1/2 cup heavy cream	1/4 cup crumbled cotija cheese
Juice of 1 lime	Fresh cilantro for garnish

Directions:

a) For roughly five minutes, or until the garlic and onion have reached the desired level of tenderness, melt the butter in a large saucepan and place it over medium heat. b) After incorporating the chilli powder and smoked paprika, continue to cook for an additional minute. c) Bring the soup to a boil after adding the corn and broth. d) To let the flavours combine, lower the heat and simmer for ten minutes. e) You may either pulse the soup for a chunkier texture or mix it until it's smooth with your Ninja Blast Max Blender. f) Add the lime juice, heavy cream, and crumbled cotija cheese, and cook for an additional five minutes. g) As necessary, add salt and pepper to taste and adjust the seasoning. h) After garnishing the soup with fresh cilantro, serve it while it is still hot.

191. Coconut Mango Chicken Curry

Total Time: 30 minutes | Prep Time: 10 minutes

Ingredients:

	1 lb chicken breast, diced
1 mango, peeled and chopped	1 cup coconut milk
1 tbsp curry powder	1 tsp ground ginger
1/2 tsp cumin	1 tbsp olive oil
Salt and pepper, to taste	

Directions:

a) Warm the olive oil in a large saucepan by heating it over a medium flame. b) Cook the chicken breast until it is browned all over. c) Mango, coconut milk, curry powder, ginger, cumin, salt, and pepper should all be blended until smooth in your Ninja Blast Max Blender. d) Stir the chicken after adding the mango mixture. e) The sauce should thicken after 10 to 15 minutes of simmering on low. f) Taste and adjust the seasoning. g) Serve with flatbread or over rice.

192. Blender Jerk Chicken Marinade

Total Time: 10 minutes | Prep Time: 10 minutes

Ingredients:

	1/2 cup soy sauce
1 tbsp olive oil	2 tbsp lime juice
1 tbsp brown sugar	1 tsp ground allspice
1/2 tsp cinnamon	1-2 scotch bonnet peppers (or to taste)
2 cloves garlic, minced	1 tsp fresh thyme

Directions:

a) Fill the Ninja Blast Max Blender with all of the ingredients. b) Blend until well mixed and smooth. c) Allow the chicken to remain in the marinade for at least two hours after covering it with the marinade. d) Bake or grill the chicken how you want. e) Add some lime and fresh cilantro as garnish.

193. Vegan Roasted Tomato Bisque

Total Time: 45 minutes | Prep Time: 10 minutes

Ingredients:

	6 large tomatoes, halved
1 onion, quartered	3 garlic cloves, peeled
2 tbsp olive oil	1/2 cup vegetable broth
1/4 cup coconut cream	Salt and pepper, to taste
Fresh basil for garnish	

Directions:

a) Set the oven's temperature to 400°F or 200°C. b) Arrange the garlic, tomatoes, and onion on a baking sheet, cover with olive oil, and roast for twenty-five minutes. c) Add the roasted veggies to the Ninja Blast Max Blender. d) Blend in veggie broth until smooth. e) After adding the bisque to a saucepan, let it boil for five to ten minutes. f) Add salt, pepper, and coconut cream and stir. g) Before serving, garnish with fresh basil.

194. Basil & Spinach Green Goddess Dressing

Total Time: 10 minutes | Prep Time: 10 minutes

Ingredients:

	1 cup fresh basil leaves
1 cup spinach leaves	1/2 cup Greek yogurt
1 tbsp lemon juice	1 tsp garlic powder
1/4 cup olive oil	Salt and pepper, to taste

Directions:

a) Fill the Ninja Blast Max Blender with the following Ingredients: basil, spinach, Greek yoghurt, lemon juice, garlic powder, olive oil, salt, and pepper. b) Blend till creamy and smooth. c) If needed, taste and adjust the seasoning. d) Keep in the refrigerator for up to a week in an airtight container. e) Serve as a dip or drizzle over salads.

195. Creamy Red Lentil Soup

Total Time: 35 minutes | Prep Time: 10 minutes

Ingredients:

	1 cup red lentils
1 onion, chopped	2 carrots, chopped
3 garlic cloves, minced	4 cups vegetable broth
1 tsp cumin	1/2 tsp turmeric
1/2 tsp smoked paprika	1 tbsp olive oil
1/4 cup coconut milk	Salt and pepper, to taste

Directions:

a) In a large saucepan, heat the olive oil over medium heat. b) Sauté the garlic, onion, and carrots for around five minutes or until they are tender. c) Stir for one minute after adding the smoked paprika, cumin, turmeric, salt, and pepper. d) Add the veggie broth and lentils. After bringing it to a boil, lower the heat and simmer the lentils for 20 minutes or until they are soft. e) In batches, move the soup to the Ninja Blast Max Blender, then process it until it's smooth. f) After adding the coconut milk, simmer for five more minutes. g) Garnish with fresh parsley and serve hot.

196. Blender Tandoori Chicken Marinade

Total Time: 20 minutes | Prep Time: 10 minutes

Ingredients:

	1 cup plain yogurt
2 tablespoons lemon juice	2 tablespoons tandoori spice mix
1 tablespoon garlic, minced	1 tablespoon ginger, minced
1 tablespoon ground cumin	1 teaspoon turmeric
1 teaspoon smoked paprika	Salt to taste
2 tablespoons olive oil	

Directions:

a) Add the yoghurt, lemon juice, olive oil, ginger, garlic, and all the spices to your Ninja Blast Max Blender. b) On high, blend until the mixture is fully blended and smooth. c) If needed, taste and adjust the seasoning. d) Cover the chicken with the marinade and toss to coat every piece. e) To enable the flavours to meld together, cover the dish and place it in the refrigerator for at least half an hour (or overnight). f) You may roast, bake, or grill your marinated chicken how you choose.

197. Honey Mustard Chicken Marinade

Total Time: 15 minutes | Prep Time: 10 minutes

Ingredients:

	3 tablespoons honey
3 tablespoons Dijon mustard	2 tablespoons olive oil
1 tablespoon apple cider vinegar	1 clove garlic, minced
Salt and pepper to taste	

Directions:

a) Put the olive oil, apple cider vinegar, honey, Dijon mustard, and chopped garlic in a blender. b) Blend until it's smooth. c) To suit your preferences, adjust the amount of salt and pepper. d) Cover the chicken thighs or breasts with the marinade. e) Make sure the chicken is well covered with marinade by tossing it. f) Refrigerate, covered, for 30 to 60 minutes before cooking.

198. Southwest Black Bean & Corn Soup

Total Time: 30 minutes | Prep Time: 10 minutes

Ingredients:

	1 can (15 oz) black beans, drained
1 can (15 oz) corn kernels, drained	1 cup vegetable broth
1/2 cup salsa	1 teaspoon cumin
1/2 teaspoon chilli powder	1/2 teaspoon smoked paprika
Salt to taste	1 tablespoon olive oil

Directions:

a) Add the black beans, corn, salsa, vegetable broth, and all the seasonings to the Ninja Blast Max Blender. b) On medium speed, blend until smooth, but leave some chunks for texture. c) After pouring the mixture into a saucepan, cook it for about ten minutes over medium heat. d) Salt and spices should be tasted and adjusted as required, with stirring occurring at regular intervals. e) Continue blending until smooth, then reheat for a creamier soup. f) With a dollop of sour cream or a garnish of cilantro, serve the dish while it is still hot.

DESSERT RECIPES

199. Creamy Chocolate Mousse

Total Time: 15 minutes | Prep Time: 10 minutes

Ingredients:

	1 cup heavy cream
1/2 cup semi-sweet chocolate chips	1 tablespoon sugar
1 teaspoon vanilla extract	Pinch of salt

Directions:

a) To melt the chocolate chips, place them in a microwave-safe dish and heat them for thirty seconds at a time, stirring them often until they get the desired consistency. b) Put the sugar, vanilla, salt, heavy cream, and melted chocolate in your blender. c) On medium, blend until the mixture thickens and takes on a creamy consistency. d) If you want it sweeter, taste and adjust the sugar. e) Transfer the mousse into bowls or serving glasses. f) Before serving, let it cool for at least an hour. Add chocolate shavings or whipped cream as a garnish.

200. Strawberry Cheesecake Shake

Total Time: 10 minutes | Prep Time: 5 minutes

Ingredients:

	1 cup fresh or frozen strawberries
1/2 cup cream cheese, softened	1 cup vanilla ice cream
1/2 cup milk	2 tablespoons honey or sugar (to taste)
1/4 teaspoon vanilla extract	

Directions:

a) Add the milk, honey (or sugar), vanilla extract, cream cheese, vanilla ice cream, and strawberries to your Ninja Blast Max Blender. b) On high, blend until creamy and smooth. c) If desired, add extra sugar or honey to taste and adjust sweetness. d) Serve right away after pouring into glasses. e) Optional: Garnish with more strawberries and whipped cream.

201. Blueberry Bliss Smoothie Bowl

Total Time: 10 minutes | Prep Time: 10 minutes

Ingredients:

	1 cup frozen blueberries
1/2 banana, sliced	1/2 cup almond milk
1 tablespoon honey or maple syrup (optional)	1/4 cup granola
1 tablespoon chia seeds	Fresh blueberries and coconut flakes for garnish (optional)

Directions:

a) Fill the Ninja Blast Max Blender with almond milk, banana, and frozen blueberries. b) On high, blend until creamy and smooth. c) In order to get the desired consistency, if the mixture is too thick, you may add a little bit more almond milk. d) If you want it sweeter, taste it and add honey or maple syrup. e) In a bowl, pour the smoothie. f) Sprinkle fresh blueberries, coconut flakes, chia seeds, and granola over top. g) Serve right away and savour!

202. Mango Coconut Pudding

Total Time: 5 minutes | Prep Time: 5 minutes

Ingredients:

	1 cup frozen mango chunks
1/2 cup coconut milk	1 tablespoon chia seeds
1 teaspoon vanilla extract	1 tablespoon honey or agave syrup (optional)

Directions:

a) In the Ninja Blast Max Blender, combine the frozen mango chunks, coconut milk, chia seeds, honey/agave, and vanilla essence. b) On high, blend until creamy and smooth. c) In the event that the mixture is too thick, continue to add additional coconut milk until the desired consistency is reached. d) If desired, taste and add extra honey or agave to adjust sweetness. e) Transfer the mixture to dishes or serving cups. f) To allow the pudding to set, place it in the refrigerator for one to two hours. g) If preferred, top with shredded coconut and serve cool.

203. Peanut Butter Banana Ice Cream

Total Time: 5 minutes | Prep Time: 5 minutes

Ingredients:

	2 ripe bananas, sliced and frozen
1/4 cup peanut butter	1/4 cup almond milk (or any milk of choice)
1/2 teaspoon vanilla extract	1 tablespoon honey or maple syrup (optional)

Directions:

a) Fill the Ninja Blast Max Blender with frozen banana slices, peanut butter, almond milk, honey/maple syrup, and vanilla extract. b) Blend until a soft-serve ice cream-like consistency is achieved. To help the blender mix evenly, you may need to scrape down the edges. c) To improve blending, add a little almond milk if the mixture is too thick. d) If necessary, adjust the sweetness with honey or maple syrup after tasting. e) For a soft-serve style, serve right away; for a firmer texture, freeze for one to two hours. f) Enjoy after scooping into bowls or cones!

204. Raspberry Chia Pudding

Total Time: 5 minutes | Prep Time: 5 minutes

Ingredients:

	1 cup frozen raspberries
1/2 cup almond milk (or any milk of choice)	1 tablespoon chia seeds
1 teaspoon maple syrup or honey (optional)	Fresh raspberries for topping (optional)

Directions:

a) Fill the Ninja Blast Max Blender with frozen raspberries, almond milk, chia seeds, and honey or maple syrup. b) On high, blend until creamy and smooth. c) Adjust the texture by adding a bit more almond milk if the combination is too thick. d) If necessary, use honey or maple syrup to modify the sweetness after tasting. e) To give the chia seeds time to expand, pour the mixture into a dish or cup and place it in the refrigerator for at least half an hour. f) Top with your preferred fruit or fresh raspberries and serve cold.

205. Vanilla Bean Protein Shake

Total Time: 5 minutes | Prep Time: 5 minutes

Ingredients:

	1 scoop vanilla protein powder
1/2 cup almond milk (or any milk of choice)	1/2 banana
1/2 teaspoon vanilla extract	1/2 teaspoon ground cinnamon (optional)
1 tablespoon honey or maple syrup (optional)	

Directions:

a) Put the banana, almond milk, vanilla protein powder, cinnamon, vanilla extract, and honey or maple syrup, if you're using it, into the Ninja

Blast Max Blender. Blend until smooth. b) Blend till creamy and smooth. c) To get the desired consistency, add more almond milk if the shake is too thick. d) Taste and, if desired, add more honey, maple syrup, or cinnamon to alter sweetness or taste. e) Pour into a shaker bottle or glass. f) Serve right now or refrigerate for later.

206. Chocolate Avocado Mousse

Total Time: 10 minutes | Prep Time: 10 minutes

Ingredients:

- 2 ripe avocados, peeled and pitted
- 1/4 cup unsweetened cocoa powder
- 1/4 cup maple syrup (or honey)
- 1 teaspoon vanilla extract
- 1/4 cup coconut milk (or almond milk)
- A pinch of salt

Directions:

a) Fill the Ninja Blast Max Blender with avocados, coconut milk, vanilla extract, maple syrup, chocolate powder, and salt. b) On high, blend until creamy and smooth. c) In order to guarantee that everything is well combined, you should pause the blender and scrape down the sides as required. d) If desired, add more maple syrup after tasting to adjust sweetness. e) Transfer the mousse to serving plates when it has been well mixed. f) Before serving, let it cool for 30 minutes. g) If desired, garnish with shaved chocolate, berries, or whipped cream.

207. Tropical Pineapple Sorbet

Total Time: 5 minutes | Prep Time: 5 minutes

Ingredients:

- 2 cups frozen pineapple chunks
- 1/2 cup coconut milk
- Juice of 1 lime
- 1 tablespoon honey or agave syrup

Directions:

a) Fill the Ninja Blast Max Blender with frozen pineapple, lime juice, coconut milk, and honey. b) When necessary, scrape down the sides of the bowl as you blend on high until the mixture is smooth and creamy. c) If you find that the mixture is too thick, you may add a little bit more coconut milk to get a smooth consistency. d) After blending, pour the sorbet onto a dish or bowl. e) To firm up, freeze for at least two hours. f) Serve with a lime slice or a sprig of mint.

208. Almond Butter Brownie Batter

Total Time: 10 minutes | Prep Time: 10 minutes

Ingredients:

- 1/2 cup almond butter
- 1/4 cup unsweetened cocoa powder
- 1/4 cup maple syrup
- 1/4 cup almond flour
- 1/2 teaspoon vanilla extract
- A pinch of salt

Directions:

a) Fill the Ninja Blast Max Blender with almond butter, chocolate powder, maple syrup, almond flour, vanilla extract, and salt. b) On high, blend until the batter is smooth and all the ingredients have been mixed. c) To properly combine the ingredients, scrape down the sides of the blender if necessary. d) If desired, add a bit extra maple syrup after tasting to balance the sweetness. e) Serve immediately, or chill for twenty minutes to allow the mixture to thicken. f) Add your preferred nuts or chocolate chips for taste.

209. Frozen Berry Yogurt Bark

Total Time: 15 minutes | Prep Time: 10 minutes | Freeze Time: 5 hours

Ingredients:

- 1 cup Greek yogurt
- 1 tablespoon honey or maple syrup
- 1/2 teaspoon vanilla extract
- 1/2 cup mixed frozen berries
- 1/4 cup granola (optional)
- 1 tablespoon shredded coconut (optional)

Directions:

a) Add the Greek yoghurt, honey, and vanilla extract to the Ninja Blast Max Blender. b) To get a smooth and creamy consistency, blend on medium speed. c) Spread the yoghurt mixture onto a parchment-lined baking sheet, forming a thin, even layer. d) Sprinkle the mixed frozen berries, granola, and shredded coconut over the yoghurt layer. e) Freeze for at least 4-5 hours or until the bark is firm. f) Once frozen, break into pieces and serve. g) Always be sure to store in an airtight container in the freezer.

210. Pumpkin Pie Smoothie

Total Time: 5 minutes | Prep Time: 5 minutes

Ingredients:

- 1/2 cup almond milk
- 1/2 cup canned pumpkin puree
- 1 frozen banana
- 1/2 teaspoon pumpkin pie spice
- 1 tablespoon maple syrup
- 1/2 teaspoon vanilla extract

Directions:

a) In the Ninja Blast Max Blender, combine the pumpkin puree, almond milk, frozen banana, pumpkin pie spice, maple syrup, and vanilla extract. Blend until smooth. b) Blend on high until smooth and creamy. c) Stop the blender and scrape the sides as necessary to make sure everything is fully blended. d) Try it out and modify the sweetness by adding additional maple syrup if you want it to be sweeter. e) In order to obtain the correct consistency, you may need to add a little bit more almond milk if the smoothie has too much liquid. f) Pour into a glass and enjoy immediately.

211. Matcha Green Tea Ice Cream

Total Time: 4 hours | Prep Time: 10 minutes

Ingredients:

- 1 cup whole milk
- 2 cups heavy cream
- 3/4 cup sugar
- 2 tbsp matcha powder
- 1 tsp vanilla extract
- Pinch of salt

Directions:

a) In the Ninja Blast Max Blender, combine the heavy cream, whole milk, sugar, matcha powder, vanilla extract, and salt. b) Blend for thirty seconds on high until the mixture is completely smooth and fully incorporated. Taste and adjust sweetness or matcha powder as needed. c) Pour the mixture into a shallow container or ice cream mould. d) Freeze for at least 4 hours or overnight to firm up. e) Before serving, let it sit at room temperature for 5 minutes to soften slightly. f) Scoop and enjoy your creamy matcha green tea ice cream!

212. Chocolate Chip Cookie Dough Dip

Total Time: 10 minutes | Prep Time: 10 minutes

Ingredients:

- 1/2 cup unsalted butter, softened

1/2 cup brown sugar	1/4 cup white sugar
1 tsp vanilla extract	1/2 cup flour (heat-treated)
1/4 tsp salt	1/2 cup mini chocolate chips
2 tbsp milk (or as needed)	

Directions:

a) The butter, brown sugar, white sugar, and vanilla extract should be blended together in the Ninja Blast Max Blender until they are completely smooth. b) Add the milk, salt, and flour to the mixture. Use a low-speed blender to mix the ingredients, scraping down the sides as necessary. c) If the dip is too thick, add a bit more milk to reach your desired consistency. d) Stir in the mini chocolate chips. e) Taste and adjust the sweetness if necessary. f) Serve with graham crackers, pretzels, or fruit for dipping. g) Enjoy your easy and indulgent cookie dough dip!

213. Banana Oatmeal Mug Cake

Total Time: 5 minutes | Prep Time: 2 minutes

Ingredients:

	1 ripe banana
1/4 cup oats	1/4 tsp baking powder
1/4 tsp cinnamon	1 tbsp maple syrup (optional)
1/4 cup milk (or non-dairy milk)	1 tbsp peanut butter (optional)

Directions:

a) In the Ninja Blast Max Blender, blend the ripe banana until smooth. b) Add the oats, baking powder, cinnamon, maple syrup, and milk, blending on medium speed until the mixture is smooth and well combined. c) Pour the mixture into a microwave-safe mug. d) Microwave on high for 1-2 minutes until the cake has risen and is set. e) If desired, swirl in some peanut butter before microwaving for extra flavour. f) Let the cake cool slightly before serving. g) Enjoy your warm, healthy banana oatmeal mug cake!

214. Mocha Frappe Delight

Total Time: 5 minutes | Prep Time: 5 minutes

Ingredients:

	1 cup brewed coffee (cooled)
1/2 cup milk (or non-dairy milk)	1 tbsp cocoa powder
2 tbsp sugar (or sweetener of choice)	1/2 tsp vanilla extract
1 cup ice	Whipped cream (optional)

Directions:

a) In the Ninja Blast Max Blender, combine the cooled coffee, milk, cocoa powder, sugar, and vanilla extract. b) Blend on high until smooth and frothy. c) Add in the ice and blend again until the drink is slushy and well-mixed. d) Taste and adjust sweetness or cocoa powder as needed. e) Pour the mixture into a glass, and if you so choose, garnish it with whipped cream. f) Serve immediately and enjoy your refreshing mocha frappe delight!

215. Nutella Banana Whip

Total Time: 5 minutes | Prep Time: 5 minutes

Ingredients:

	2 ripe bananas
2 tbsp Nutella	1/4 cup milk (or non-dairy milk)
1/4 tsp vanilla extract	Ice cubes (optional)

Directions:

a) In the Ninja Blast Max Blender, blend the ripe bananas until smooth. b) The Nutella, milk, and vanilla extract should be added to the blender, and the mixture should be blended on medium speed until it is completely incorporated. c) If you want the consistency to be more thick, add a few ice cubes and combine them once more. Taste and adjust the sweetness if needed. d) Pour into a glass or bowl and serve immediately. e) Enjoy your creamy, dreamy Nutella banana whip!

216. Salted Caramel Protein Shake

Total Time: 5 minutes | Prep Time: 5 minutes

Ingredients:

- 1 tablespoon caramel syrup
- 1 cup unsweetened almond milk
- 1/2 teaspoon vanilla extract
- 1 scoop vanilla protein powder
- 1/2 teaspoon sea salt
- 1/2 frozen banana
- Ice cubes (optional)

Directions:

a) Add the vanilla protein powder, caramel syrup, sea salt, almond milk, banana, and vanilla extract to the Ninja Blast Max Blender. b) To get a smooth and creamy consistency, blend on medium speed. c) If you want the consistency to be more substantial, you may add ice cubes and combine the mixture once more. Taste and adjust sweetness or saltiness if needed by adding more syrup or salt. d) After the shake has been poured into a glass, a small amount of sea salt should be sprinkled on top as a garnish. e) Serve immediately for a satisfying, salty-sweet boost!

217. Blackberry Coconut Cream Bars

Total Time: 2 hours 15 minutes | Prep Time: 15 minutes

Ingredients:

- 1 cup almond flour
- 1/2 cup coconut oil, melted
- 1/4 cup coconut milk
- 1/4 teaspoon vanilla extract
- 1 cup dried coconut flakes
- 1/4 cup maple syrup
- 1 cup fresh or frozen blackberries
- 1 tablespoon honey

Directions:

a) In the Ninja Blast Max Blender, combine coconut flakes, almond flour, maple syrup, and melted coconut oil. b) The mixture should be blended until it resembles dough, and then it should be pressed into the bottom of a baking dish that has been lined. c) In a separate bowl, blend blackberries, coconut milk, honey, and vanilla extract until smooth. d) Pour the blackberry mixture over the coconut crust and spread evenly. e) Freeze the bars for 2 hours to set. f) Once firm, slice into squares or bars. g) Serve chilled as a refreshing, creamy treat.

218. Chocolate Hazelnut Spread

Total Time: 10 minute | Prep Time: 10 minutes

Ingredients:

- 1/4 cup cocoa powder
- 1/4 cup coconut oil, melted
- Pinch of sea salt
- 1 cup roasted hazelnuts
- 1/4 cup maple syrup
- 1 teaspoon vanilla extract

Directions:

a) After the hazelnuts have been roasted, place them in the Ninja Blast Max Blender and process them until they make a smooth paste. b) Include the cocoa powder, maple syrup, melted coconut oil, vanilla essence, and salt from the sea in the preparation. c) Repeat the process of blending until all of the components are completely combined and the spread is seamless. d) If you want to change the sweetness or saltiness of the dish, you may taste it and add additional maple syrup or salt instead. e) Place the spread in a jar or another container that can seal the air out. f) Refrigerate for up to two weeks after it has been prepared. As a dip, on toast, or on fruit, you may enjoy it!

219. Honey Almond Date Balls

Total Time: 15 minutes | Prep Time: 15 minutes

Ingredients:

1 cup pitted dates	1 cup almonds
1 teaspoon vanilla extract	1/4 cup honey
1 tablespoon chia seeds (optional)	1/4 teaspoon sea salt

Directions:

a) Add almonds and dates to the Ninja Blast Max Blender and pulse until finely chopped. b) Add honey, vanilla extract, sea salt, and chia seeds (if using). c) Blend at low speed, scraping the sides if necessary, until sticky dough forms. d) Create bite-sized balls out of the dough by rolling it out with your hands until it is at the desired size. e) Refrigerate the balls for fifteen minutes in order to firm them up. Place them on a pan that has been lined with parchment paper. Serve as a quick snack or energy boost.

220. Key Lime Pie Smoothie

Total Time: 5 minutes | Prep Time: 5 minutes

Ingredients:

1/2 cup unsweetened almond milk	1/2 cup plain Greek yogurt
	1/4 cup fresh lime juice
1 tablespoon honey	1/2 avocado
1/4 teaspoon lime zest	Ice cubes (optional)

Directions:

a) Add Greek yoghurt, almond milk, lime juice, honey, avocado, and lime zest to the Ninja Blast Max Blender. b) Blend on high until the mixture is silky smooth and creamy. c) If you would want your smoothie to be cooler, you may add a handful of ice cubes and combine it once more. d) You may alter the sweetness by tasting it and adding additional honey if you want to. e) Pour the mixture into a glass, and then garnish it with more lime zest or a slice of lime. f) Serve immediately and enjoy the refreshing, tangy flavour!

221. Cinnamon Apple Crumble Shake

Total Time: 10 minutes | Prep Time: 10 minutes

Ingredients:

	1 large apple, peeled and diced
1/2 cup vanilla yogurt	1/2 cup almond milk (or milk of choice)
1/2 tsp ground cinnamon	1/4 cup rolled oats
1 tbsp honey (optional)	1/2 cup ice cubes

Directions:

a) Add the diced apple, vanilla yoghurt, almond milk, ground cinnamon, and rolled oats into the Ninja Blast Max blender. b) Drizzle in the honey if desired. c) Add the ice cubes to the blender. d) Blend on high for 30-45 seconds or until smooth and creamy. e) Taste and adjust sweetness, adding more honey if needed. f) Pour the shake into a glass and top with a sprinkle of cinnamon or granola for added crunch. g) Serve immediately and enjoy your delicious, creamy shake!

222. Espresso Chocolate Pudding

Total Time: 15 minutes | Prep Time: 15 minutes

Ingredients:

	1/2 cup heavy cream
1/2 cup milk	1/4 cup sugar
2 tbsp unsweetened cocoa powder	1 shot of espresso
1/4 tsp vanilla extract	2 tbsp cornstarch

Directions:

a) Milk, heavy cream, sugar, cocoa powder, and espresso should be mixed together in a small pot first. b) By continuously whisking the mixture while heating it over medium-low heat, the liquid should become warm but not boiling. c) It is necessary to create a slurry by combining cornstarch with a tiny amount of water in a small bowl. d) Slowly pour the slurry into the warm mixture, whisking continuously to avoid lumps. e) Continue to cook for 2-3 minutes until the pudding thickens. f) After taking the pan off the heat, whisk in the vanilla essence. g) Pour the pudding into serving cups and let it cool to room temperature, then refrigerate for at least 1 hour before serving. h) If you so wish, you may finish it off with chocolate shavings or whipped cream.

223. Pineapple Coconut Snow Cream

Total Time: 10 minutes | Prep Time: 10 minutes

Ingredients:

	2 cups frozen pineapple chunks
1/2 cup coconut milk	1 tbsp honey or agave syrup (optional)
1/4 cup shredded coconut (optional for garnish)	

Directions:

a) Add the frozen pineapple chunks, coconut milk, and honey (if using) into the Ninja Blast Max blender. b) Blend on high for 30-45 seconds until smooth and creamy. c) If needed, scrape down the sides of the blender and continue blending. d) Once the mixture reaches a soft, snow-like consistency, stop blending. e) Spoon the snow cream into bowls or glasses. f) In order to provide an additional touch of the tropics, garnish with shredded coconut. g) Serve immediately for the best texture. h) Enjoy your refreshing, tropical snow cream!

224. Frozen Strawberry Lemonade Slush

Total Time: 5 minutes | Prep Time: 5 minutes

Ingredients:

	1 1/2 cups frozen strawberries
1/2 cup fresh lemon juice	1 tbsp honey or sugar (optional)
1/2 cup cold water	1 cup ice cubes

Directions:

a) Combine the frozen strawberries, lemon juice, honey (if using), and cold water into the Ninja Blast Max blender. b) Add the ice cubes to the blender. c) Blend on high for 30-45 seconds or until the mixture is slushy and smooth. d) Taste the slush and adjust the sweetness by adding more honey or sugar if needed. e) Pour the slush into glasses. f) Garnish with a fresh strawberry or lemon slice on top. g) Serve immediately and enjoy this refreshing treat on a hot day!

225. Dark Chocolate Raspberry Mousse

Total Time: 20 minutes | Prep Time: 20 minutes

Ingredients:

	1/2 cup dark chocolate

1/2 cup heavy cream

1 tbsp sugar (optional)

1/4 cup whipped cream for topping (optional)

1/2 cup fresh raspberries

1/4 tsp vanilla extract

Directions:

a) When the dark chocolate is completely melted, stir it every thirty seconds in a heatproof dish that is placed over a saucepan of boiling water (the double boiler technique) or in the microwave. b) The melted chocolate should be allowed to gently cool down while the cream is being whipped. c) To get firm peaks, whisk the heavy cream and sugar (if used) in a separate dish until they reach the desired consistency. d) The melted chocolate and vanilla extract should be added to the whipped cream, and then the mixture should be gently folded until it is completely incorporated. e) The fresh raspberries should be blended in the Ninja Blast Max blender for ten to fifteen seconds until they are completely smooth. f) Fold the raspberries that have been pureed into the mousse mixture in a gentle manner. g) The mousse should be poured into serving cups or glasses using a spoon. h) Refrigerate for 1-2 hours to allow the mousse to set, and top with whipped cream or more fresh raspberries before serving.

226. Protein-Packed Brownie Batter Dip

Total Time: 10 minutes | Prep Time: 10 minutes

Ingredients:

1/4 cup almond butter

2 tbsp honey

1 scoop of chocolate protein powder

1 cup Greek yogurt

1/4 cup cocoa powder

1 tsp vanilla extract

2 tbsp chocolate chips (optional)

Directions:

a) Fill the Ninja Blast Max Blender with Greek yoghurt, almond butter, chocolate powder, honey, and vanilla extract. b) Blend on medium speed after adding the chocolate protein powder until it's smooth. c) After the blender has been stopped, you should, if required, scrape off the sides of the blender. d) To completely mix the ingredients, blend one more for ten to fifteen seconds. e) If you want the dip sweeter, taste it and add more honey. f) If desired, add chocolate chips and stir. g) Serve with pretzels for dipping, graham crackers, or fruit.

227. Gingerbread Cookie Smoothie

Total Time: 5 minutes | Prep Time: 5 minutes

Ingredients:

1/2 cup almond milk (or milk of choice)

1/4 tsp ground ginger

1/4 tsp vanilla extract

1 tbsp chia seeds (optional)

1 frozen banana

1/4 cup rolled oats

1/4 tsp ground cinnamon

1 tsp molasses

Directions:

a) In the blender, combine the ground ginger, oats, almond milk, molasses, cinnamon, ground banana, and vanilla essence. b) On high, blend until the mixture is creamy and smooth. c) Blend again after adding a bit more almond milk if the smoothie is too thick. d) If you want more fibre, add chia seeds and mix once more. e) If additional molasses is needed, taste and adjust the sweetness. f) Transfer to a glass and serve right away.

228. Carrot Cake Bliss Balls

Total Time: 10 minutes | Prep Time: 10 minutes

Ingredients:

1/2 cup shredded carrots	1 cup rolled oats
1/4 cup raisins	1/4 cup almond flour
1/2 tsp ground cinnamon	1/4 cup unsweetened shredded coconut
2 tbsp honey or maple syrup	1/2 tsp ground ginger
	1 tbsp coconut oil

Directions:

a) In the blender, combine the oats, almond flour, raisins, shredded coconut, ginger, cinnamon, and carrot shreds. b) Blend until all ingredients are blended and chopped coarsely. c) Add coconut oil and honey or maple syrup. d) Pulse until, when pushed, the mixture holds together. e) Using your hands, roll the mixture into little balls. f) To firm up, place the balls on a dish and place them in the refrigerator for half an hour. g) Savour it as a nutritious treat or as a fast snack!

229. Creamy Coconut Rice Pudding

Total Time: 15 minutes | Prep Time: 5 minutes

Ingredients:

1 cup coconut milk	1/2 cup cooked white rice
1/4 tsp ground cinnamon	1/4 cup honey or maple syrup
1 tbsp shredded coconut (for garnish)	1/4 tsp vanilla extract

Directions:

a) In the blender, combine the cooked rice, coconut milk, honey, cinnamon, and vanilla essence. b) On medium, blend until creamy and smooth. c) To get the required consistency, add more coconut milk if the pudding is too thick. d) Transfer the pudding onto a serving dish or bowl. e) Add some texture by garnishing with shredded coconut. f) Before serving, chill in the refrigerator for ten minutes, or eat right away.

230. Chocolate Covered Cherry Shake

Total Time: 5 minutes | Prep Time: 5 minutes

Ingredients:

1/2 cup milk of choice	1 cup frozen cherries
1 tbsp honey or maple syrup	1 tbsp cocoa powder
1/4 cup Greek yoghurt (optional for creaminess)	1/2 tsp vanilla extract
	2 tbsp dark chocolate chips (for garnish)

Directions:

a) Fill the blender with milk, cocoa powder, honey, frozen cherries, and vanilla essence. b) On high, blend until creamy and smooth. c) Blend again after adding Greek yoghurt if you like a thicker shake. d) If necessary, taste and add additional honey to adjust sweetness. e) Fill a glass with the shake. f) Add dark chocolate chips as a garnish. g) Savour the rich, chocolaty taste right away!

231. Mango Passionfruit Sorbet

Total Time: 10 minutes | Prep Time: 10 minutes

Ingredients:

1/2 cup frozen passionfruit pulp	2 ripe mangoes, peeled and cubed
1/2 cup coconut water	1 tablespoon honey or agave syrup (optional)

Directions:

a) In the Ninja Blast Max Blender, combine the mango cubes, passionfruit pulp, and honey. b) Fill the blender with 1/2 cup of coconut water. c) Blend until smooth and creamy, about 30 seconds on high. d) Add additional coconut water if the mixture is too thick until the right consistency is reached. e) If desired, taste and add additional honey to adjust sweetness. f) For a soft-serve texture, serve right away; for a harder sorbet, freeze for one to two hours. g) Enjoy after scooping into bowls!

232. Oatmeal Raisin Cookie Dough Bites

Total Time: 15 minutes | Prep Time: 10 minutes

Ingredients:

1 1/2 cups rolled oats

1/4 cup peanut butter

1/4 cup honey or maple syrup

1/4 cup raisins

1 teaspoon vanilla extract

Pinch of salt

Directions:

a) In the Ninja Blast Max Blender, combine the oats, peanut butter, honey, vanilla extract, and salt. b) Until everything is fully blended, blend on medium speed for 15 to 20 seconds. c) When necessary, pause to scrape down the blender's sides. d) Pulse just long enough to include the raisins. e) Using your hands, roll the dough into bite-sized balls. f) Arrange the cookie dough pieces on a parchment paper-lined pan. g) For a firmer texture, refrigerate for 10 minutes before serving.

233. Chocolate Covered Almond Shake

Total Time: 5 minutes | Prep Time: 5 minutes

Ingredients:

1 cup unsweetened almond milk

1/2 cup frozen banana slices

2 tablespoons almond butter

1/4 cup whole almonds (optional for crunch)

1 tablespoon unsweetened cocoa powder

1 tablespoon maple syrup

Directions:

a) In the Ninja Blast Max Blender, mix together almond milk, banana, chocolate powder, almond butter, and maple syrup. b) Blend until smooth, 30 seconds on high. c) If desired, add whole almonds and pulse just enough to integrate them for extra texture. d) Transfer to a glass and serve right away. e) Drizzle with melted chocolate for added decadence.

234. Peanut Butter Fudge Swirl

Total Time: 10 minutes | Prep Time: 10 minutes

Ingredients:

1/4 cup unsweetened almond milk

1/2 teaspoon vanilla extract

1/2 cup peanut butter

1 tablespoon maple syrup

Pinch of sea salt

Directions:

a) Fill the Ninja Blast Max Blender with peanut butter, almond milk, maple syrup, vanilla essence, and sea salt. b) Blend till smooth and creamy, 30 seconds on high. c) If necessary, add extra maple syrup to balance the mixture's sweetness after tasting it. d) The fudge mixture should be transferred to a small container. e) Put it in the fridge for around two hours or until it solidifies to the consistency of fudge. f) Cut into squares and dig in!

235. Lemon Blueberry Parfait

Total Time: 10 minutes | Prep Time: 10 minutes

Ingredients:

	1 cup frozen blueberries
1/2 cup Greek yoghurt (or dairy-free alternative)	1 tablespoon honey or agave syrup
1 tablespoon lemon juice	1/2 teaspoon lemon zest
1/4 cup granola (for topping)	

Directions:

a) Fill the Ninja Blast Max Blender with frozen blueberries, Greek yoghurt, honey, lemon juice, and lemon zest. b) Blend till smooth and creamy, 30 seconds on high. c) If necessary, taste and adjust the sweetness or lemon flavour. d) Fill serving glasses with the blueberry yoghurt mixture using a spoon. e) For crunch, sprinkle more fresh blueberries and oats on top. f) Serve right now or chill until you're ready to eat.

236. Chocolate Mint Chip Shake

Total Time: 5 minutes | Prep Time: 5 minutes

Ingredients:

	1 cup almond milk (or milk of choice)
1 frozen banana	1/2 cup spinach (optional for green colour)
2 tbsp cocoa powder	1/4 tsp peppermint extract
1 tbsp mini chocolate chips	1 tbsp honey (or sweetener of choice)

Directions:

a) In the blender, combine the frozen banana and almond milk. b) Add the honey, peppermint essence, cocoa powder, and spinach if using. c) On high, blend until creamy and smooth. d) Following the completion of the blending process, the chocolate chips should be added and then pulsed several times in order to combine them. e) If preferred, top with a mint leaf or more chocolate chips after pouring into a glass. f) Serve right away and savour!

237. Caramel Apple Pie Smoothie

Total Time: 5 minutes | Prep Time: 5 minutes

Ingredients:

	1 medium apple, peeled and chopped
1/2 cup Greek yogurt	1/4 cup almond milk
1 tbsp caramel sauce	1/2 tsp cinnamon
1/4 tsp nutmeg	Ice cubes (optional for thicker texture)

Directions:

a) In the blender, combine the diced apple, Greek yoghurt, almond milk, and caramel sauce. b) For an apple pie taste, add nutmeg and cinnamon. c) Blend until smooth, adding ice cubes if a thicker texture is preferred. d) If necessary, add extra caramel or spices after tasting. e) Transfer to a glass. f) Add a piece of apple to the rim or a dusting of cinnamon as a garnish. g) Serve right away and savour!

238. Toasted Coconut Cream Shake

Total Time: 5 minutes | Prep Time: 5 minutes

Ingredients:

	1/2 cup coconut milk
1 frozen banana	1/4 cup shredded coconut, toasted

1 tsp vanilla extract

1 tbsp honey or maple syrup

1/2 cup ice (optional for texture)

Directions:

a) Toasting the shredded coconut in a pan over medium heat for two to three minutes, or until it is golden brown and fragrant, is the recommended method. b) In the blender, combine the toasted coconut, frozen banana, and coconut milk. c) Add honey or maple syrup and vanilla essence. d) Blend until smooth, adding ice if desired for a colder shake. e) Transfer to a glass and garnish with more toasted coconut. f) Serve right away and savour!

239. Chocolate Espresso Energy Balls

Total Time: 10 minutes | Prep Time: 10 minutes

Ingredients:

	1 cup dates, pitted
1/2 cup almonds	2 tbsp cocoa powder
1 tbsp espresso powder	1 tbsp chia seeds (optional)
Pinch of salt	1/4 cup chocolate chips

Directions:

a) Pulse the dates and almonds in the blender until they are minced and mixed together. b) Stir in chia seeds, espresso powder, cocoa powder, and a dash of salt. c) Ongoing mixing should be continued until the mixture begins to come together. d) Pulse a couple of times to mix in the chocolate chips. e) Using a spoon, form the mixture into little balls that are approximately 1 inch around. f) At this point, the balls should be placed on a baking sheet that has been lined with parchment paper and then placed in the refrigerator for half an hour. Keep in the refrigerator for up to a week in an airtight container.

240. Vanilla Almond Butter Mousse

Total Time: 5 minutes | Prep Time: 5 minutes

Ingredients:

	1 cup heavy cream or coconut cream
1/4 cup almond butter	1 tsp vanilla extract
1 tbsp maple syrup	Pinch of salt

Directions:

a) Put heavy cream, almond butter, maple syrup, and vanilla extract in a blender. b) For added taste, add a pinch of salt. c) Blend until frothy and mousse-like, approximately 2 to 3 minutes on high. d) If extra maple syrup is needed, taste and adjust the sweetness. e) Transfer to glasses or a few serving dishes. f) Before serving, let the mousse set in the refrigerator for ten to fifteen minutes. g) If preferred, garnish with chopped berries or almonds, then dig in!

241. Dark Chocolate Peanut Butter Cups

Total Time: 1 hour | Prep Time: 10 minutes

Ingredients:

	1 cup dark chocolate chips
1/2 cup peanut butter	1 tablespoon honey
1/2 teaspoon vanilla extract	A pinch of sea salt

Directions:

a) In a container that can be used in the microwave, melt the dark chocolate chips in increments of thirty seconds while stirring them in between each one. Continue doing this until the chips are completely smooth. b) Use paper liners to line a muffin tray. c) Evenly distribute a little bit of melted chocolate in each muffin cup using a spoon. To set, put the tray in the freezer for ten minutes. d) In the Ninja Blast Max, combine peanut butter, honey, vanilla essence, and sea salt until creamy while the chocolate is hardening. e) When the chocolate has achieved its desired consistency, place the peanut butter mixture on top of it using a spoon. f) The leftover chocolate that has been melted should be spread over the top of each cup. g) Freeze until completely set, at least 30 minutes. h) When the cups are set, take them out of the muffin tray and start eating!

242. Strawberry Shortcake Smoothie

Total Time: 5 minutes | Prep Time: 5 minutes

Ingredients:

- 1 cup frozen strawberries
- 1/2 cup vanilla Greek yoghurt
- 1/2 cup almond milk
- 1 tablespoon honey
- 1/2 teaspoon vanilla extract
- Ice (optional for a thicker texture)

Directions:

a) Fill the Ninja Blast Max Blender with frozen strawberries, almond milk, honey, vanilla yoghurt, and vanilla essence. b) If you want a thicker consistency, you may add ice after blending until smooth. c) If necessary, add additional honey after tasting to regulate the sweetness. d) For an added shortcake touch, top with crumbled graham crackers or fresh strawberries after pouring into a glass. e) Serve right away and savour!

243. Maple Pecan Pie Shake

Total Time: 5 minutes | Prep Time: 5 minutes

Ingredients:

- 1 cup vanilla ice cream
- 1/2 cup milk
- 2 tablespoons maple syrup
- A pinch of salt
- 1/4 cup chopped pecans
- 1/4 teaspoon cinnamon

Directions:

a) Add the milk, chopped pecans, maple syrup, cinnamon, salt, and vanilla ice cream to the Ninja Blast Max Blender. b) Blend till creamy and smooth. c) If needed, add more maple syrup to taste and adjust sweetness. d) Transfer the drink to a glass and sprinkle some more chopped pecans on top. e) For a nutty, sweet delight, serve right away.

244. Mocha Almond Fudge Ice Cream

Total Time: 30 minutes | Prep Time: 5 minutes

Ingredients:

- 1 cup heavy cream
- 1/2 cup milk
- 2 tablespoons instant coffee granules
- 1/4 cup cocoa powder
- 1/4 cup sugar
- 1/2 cup crushed almonds
- 1/4 cup chocolate chips

Directions:

a) Dissolve the instant coffee granules in warm milk in a small dish. b) Fill the Ninja Blast Max with sugar, cocoa powder, and heavy cream. c) After adding the coffee-milk combination, blend until everything is well blended. d) Add the chocolate chips and crushed almonds and stir. e) The mixture should be transferred to a loaf pan or an ice cream container. f) Freeze until solid, 2 to 3 hours. g) For a rich, creamy delight, scoop and serve right away.

245. Coconut Chia Pudding with Berries

Total Time: 4 hours | Prep Time: 5 minutes

Ingredients:

3 tablespoons chia seeds	1 cup coconut milk
	1 tablespoon honey
1/2 teaspoon vanilla extract	1/2 cup mixed berries (strawberries, blueberries, raspberries)

Directions:

a) Combine the coconut milk, chia seeds, honey, and vanilla essence in a bowl. b) After thoroughly stirring the mixture, covering it, and placing it in the refrigerator for at least four hours or overnight, the chia seeds will have had sufficient time to absorb the liquid. c) To guarantee a smooth texture, stir the pudding one more once it has set. d) Transfer the chia pudding with a spoon into glasses or serving dishes. e) Add some fresh mixed berries on top. f) Enjoy this nutritious, creamy dessert or snack cold.

246. White Chocolate Raspberry Swirl

Total Time: 10 minutes | Prep Time: 10 minutes

Ingredients:

	1 cup frozen raspberries
1/2 cup white chocolate chips	1/2 cup Greek yogurt
1/4 cup almond milk	1 tbsp honey (optional)

Directions:

a) Add Greek yoghurt, almond milk, white chocolate chips, and frozen raspberries to your Ninja Blast Max Blender. b) Blend until smooth, 30 to 45 seconds on medium speed. c) If you want more sweetness, add honey and mix for an additional five seconds. d) To make sure everything is completely combined, scrape down the sides of the blender. e) Transfer to glasses or serving dishes. f) If desired, swirl in more melted white chocolate or raspberry puree. g) Serve right away and savour!

247. Chocolate Covered Strawberry Mousse

Total Time: 10 minutes | Prep Time: 10 minutes

Ingredients:

	1 cup frozen strawberries
1/2 cup heavy cream	1/2 cup chocolate chips
1 tbsp vanilla extract	2 tbsp honey or maple syrup

Directions:

a) Melt the chocolate chips in a small saucepan over low heat, stirring all the while. After melting, let it cool a little. b) Put the frozen strawberries, heavy cream, honey/maple syrup, and vanilla extract in your Ninja Blast Max Blender. c) Blend until smooth, 30 seconds on high. d) Add the melted chocolate gradually while mixing, then blend for ten more seconds. e) To make sure everything is combined, scrape down the sides of the blender and blend for a further five seconds. f) Transfer the mousse with a spoon into separate dishes or cups. g) Serve cold after an hour in the fridge to solidify.

248. Snickerdoodle Smoothie

Total Time: 5 minutes | Prep Time: 5 minutes

Ingredients:

	1 frozen banana
1/2 cup almond milk	1/2 tsp cinnamon
1/4 tsp vanilla extract	1 tbsp almond butter
1 tbsp honey	

Directions:

a) Fill the Ninja Blast Max Blender with the frozen banana, almond milk, honey, almond butter, cinnamon, and vanilla extract. b) Blend until smooth and creamy, about 30 seconds on high. c) If required, scrape down the blender's sides before blending for an additional five seconds. d) Transfer to a large glass. e) If desired, add some cinnamon on top as a garnish. f) Serve right away and savour the warm Snickerdoodle flavour.

249. Spiced Pumpkin Protein Pudding

Total Time: 5 minutes | Prep Time: 5 minutes

Ingredients:

	1/2 cup pumpkin puree
1/2 cup Greek yogurt	1/4 cup vanilla protein powder
1/2 tsp cinnamon	1/4 tsp nutmeg
1 tbsp maple syrup	1/4 cup almond milk

Directions:

a) Fill your Ninja Blast Max Blender with pumpkin puree, almond milk, Greek yoghurt, protein powder, cinnamon, nutmeg, and maple syrup. b) For 20 to 30 seconds, blend on high until everything is creamy and smooth. c) If needed, scrape down the edges and mix for an additional five seconds. d) Transfer to glasses or little bowls. e) To help the pudding solidify, place it in the refrigerator for one to two hours. f) Before serving, sprinkle some more cinnamon or a dollop of whipped cream on top.

250. Birthday Cake Blender Ice Cream

Total Time: 15 minutes | Prep Time: 15 minutes

Ingredients:

	2 cups frozen vanilla ice cream
1/2 cup milk	1/4 cup sprinkles
1/2 tsp vanilla extract	1 tbsp almond flour (optional for texture)

Directions:

a) Add the milk, vanilla essence, and frozen vanilla ice cream to the Ninja Blast Max Blender. b) Blend until smooth and creamy, about 30 seconds on high. c) Add additional milk, one tablespoon at a time, if the mixture is too thick until the consistency you want is achieved. d) For more taste and texture, mix in the almond flour and sprinkles. e) Transfer the ice cream onto dishes or serving glasses. f) For a firmer texture, freeze for one to two hours or serve right away as soft-serve. g) Savour this delight inspired by a birthday cake!

251. Chocolate Orange Mousse

Total Time: 15 minutes | Prep Time: 15 minutes

Ingredients:

	1 cup heavy cream
2 tbsp unsweetened cocoa powder	1/2 cup orange juice
1/4 cup powdered sugar	1 tsp orange zest
1 tsp vanilla extract	A pinch of salt

Directions:

a) Add heavy cream, powdered sugar, cocoa powder, vanilla extract, and salt to the Ninja Blast Max Blender. b) To mix the ingredients, blend on low speed for 30 seconds. c) After adding the orange juice and zest, blend the mixture once more on medium speed for one minute or until it thickens and becomes smooth. d) Make sure it's creamy in consistency. Blend for an additional 30 seconds if you want a stiffer mousse. e) For optimal results, pour the mousse into serving glasses and chill for at least an hour. f) Before serving, garnish with more orange zest or chocolate shavings. g) Serve cold.

252. Cherry Almond Bliss Shake

Total Time: 5 minutes | Prep Time: 5 minutes

Ingredients:

- 1/2 cup almond milk
- 1 tbsp almond butter
- A pinch of cinnamon
- 1 cup frozen cherries
- 1/2 cup vanilla yogurt
- 1 tbsp honey

Directions:

a) In the blender, combine the almond butter, honey, cinnamon, almond milk, vanilla yoghurt, and frozen cherries. b) For 30 to 45 seconds, blend on high until everything is creamy and smooth. c) If necessary, add additional honey after tasting to regulate the sweetness. d) Fill a glass with the shake. e) Add a cherry or a scattering of ground almonds as a garnish. f) Serve right away and savour!

253. Caramel Mocha Fudge Shake

Total Time: 7 minutes | Prep Time: 7 minutes

Ingredients:

- 1/2 cup milk (or milk alternative)
- 1 tbsp cocoa powder
- 1/2 cup ice cubes
- Drizzle of caramel sauce (for garnish)
- 1 cup brewed coffee (cooled)
- 1/4 cup caramel sauce
- 1 scoop chocolate protein powder (optional)
- Whipped cream (for garnish)

Directions:

a) In the blender, combine the brewed coffee, milk, caramel sauce, ice cubes, cocoa powder, and chocolate protein powder (if using). b) Blend until smooth, 30 to 45 seconds on high. c) If desired, add extra honey or caramel sauce after tasting to change the sweetness. d) Fill a glass with the shake. e) Add a dollop of caramel sauce and whipped cream on top. f) For a rich coffee and chocolate pleasure, serve right away!

THE END

Printed in Dunstable, United Kingdom

64496519R00051